UNITED METHODIST BELIEFS

09 10
— —
1 1

D0972214

UNITED METHODIST BELIEFS

A Brief Introduction

William H. Willimon

Westminster John Knox Press
LOUISVILLE • LONDON

Scripture quotations from the New Revised Standard Version of the Bible are copyright © 1989 by the Division of Christian Education of the National Council of the Churches of Christ in the U.S.A. and are used by permission.

Book design by Sharon Adams
Cover design by Night & Day Design

First edition
Published by Westminster John Knox Press
Louisville, Kentucky

This book is printed on acid-free paper that meets the American National Standards Institute Z39.48 standard. ∞

PRINTED IN THE UNITED STATES OF AMERICA

07 08 09 10 11 12 13 14 15 16 — 10 9 8 7 6 5 4 3 2

Library of Congress Cataloging-in-Publication Data

Willimon, William H.
　　United Methodist beliefs : a brief introduction / William H. Willimon. — 1st ed.
　　　　p. cm.
Includes bibliographical references and index.
ISBN-13: 978-0-664-23040-1 (alk. paper)
ISBN-10: 0-664-23040-7 (alk. paper)
1. United Methodist Church (U.S.)—Doctrines. I. Title.

BX9175.3 .M35 2003
230'.51—dc21

2002192709

To
Richard P. Heitzenrater
Wesleyan teacher and friend

Contents

Introduction and Warning

Follow me!"

Jesus did not say, "Believe the following six things about me" or "Follow these ten truths." In the Gospels, Jesus calls people to a journey with him, not a seminar about him. He was a prophet preaching, always on the move, constantly drawing people into his journey; he was itinerant, truth in motion; not a professor lecturing a classroom of passive, static spectators.

Even when Jesus rarely mentions belief, he isn't talking about a head trip, a set of cool intellectual propositions. He is talking about an engaging, costly relationship. "Believe in me," he says. Not "Believe these assertions about me," but rather give in, be engaged, walk with me. "I am the way, the truth, and the life," he says. Not "I am someone who tells you some truths about the way," but rather "I am the way." He is life. So the Gospels portray the disciples of Jesus as pilgrims on the way from here to there, having a hard time keeping up. When he taught, Jesus taught peripatetically, on the go rather than having everyone sit down and quietly meditate.

Jesus' first disciples, when they believed things about him, were usually wrong. The first disciples are not those who had the right thoughts about Jesus but rather those who had the guts to get into the boat and sail with him even when they didn't completely understand him. What does that tell you?

This is my somewhat anxious introduction to a book on what United Methodists believe. It is not a book of correct, official propositions (though I'll be working directly from the United

/ ix

Methodist statements of doctrine in our *Book of Discipline*—those statements are found in boldface italics in the text); instead, it is a commentary, in plain speech, of what United Methodists think we're thinking when we think about the God who is Father, Son, and Holy Spirit.[1] Our beliefs are not our intellectual achievement but rather gracious gifts that God has given us. These doctrines are guideposts along the Wesleyan way.

That I put the matter in this active, practical way—stressing discipleship along with believing, following along with thinking—is a sure sign that the Methodists have got me, evidence that I'm believing like a Wesleyan, thinking like a Methodist. Our church arises out of a revival that was launched by Church of England priests, John Wesley and his brother Charles, a small-group, lay-renewal effort to enliven the Anglican church that eventually became a new church, one of the largest Protestant denominations in the world. That revival was as much intellectual and theological as it was emotional and organizational.

Today, many who are concerned about church growth and church renewal portray Wesley as the great evangelist, who shrank the gospel into a form that could be accepted by the English masses. This is a misreading of Wesley. Although he was an evangelist, no one ever accused Wesley of theological reductionism or an attempt to distill the faith into a well-packaged "message" that people could easily comprehend and affirm.[2] While that strategy is beloved by many contemporary evangelists, it has little to do with Wesley. He was an evangelist and a leader in renewal who led by stimulating theological debate and careful, at-times-complicated theological articulation in service to a complex, unfailingly and fully orthodox view of God. In his sermons and his avalanche of books and articles Wesley encouraged people to climb up to robust Christian orthodoxy; he did not condescendingly abridge the faith to suit the limits of the unlettered masses. Few would dispute that Wesley became one of the greatest Anglican theologians of his century.

Wesley helped the church think its way through such intellectual challenges as the European Enlightenment, with its exaltation of human reason and its prejudice against the miraculous. He had to negotiate between the Protestant Reformation's insistence on

Scripture as the sole authority for faith and practice and the Catholic Counter-Reformation's entrenchment of ecclesiastical authoritarianism. He was intensely curious—to the point of quackery—about the new faith in science and technology, but he was also astutely critical. He knew of the then-new idea of human progress and many of the other "faiths" that presented intellectual alternatives to traditional Christian believing, but he rigorously adhered to the core of ancient, historic orthodoxy. Fortunately, he loved to pair seemingly contradictory and conflicting ideas in his own thinking, earning him a reputation as an eclectic, sometimes-quirky, but undeniably creative thinker. His fertile mind was constantly stoked by his being an inveterate and prodigious reader, and he dictatorially insisted that all of his lay "traveling preachers" be avaricious readers as well.

Methodism was named on a university campus when John Wesley was teaching at Oxford in the 1730s. Critics derided Wesley's followers for their systematic, rule-driven approach to being Christians, calling them mere "methodists." They also accused Wesley of advocating a "new method" of salvation (specifically, Arminianism—more about that later). Taking their slurs as a compliment, Wesley believed that there were some things that were too important to be left to only those times when you feel like doing them. He felt that a methodical, systematic approach was helpful though at times Wesley appeared somewhat compulsive in his relentless commendation of his rules and disciplines to his fledgling Methodist movement.

To be truthful, many of our fellow Christians regard the phrase "Methodist beliefs" as an oxymoron. We Methodists, as heirs of Protestant pietism, are not well known nor widely admired for our theology. Presbyterians and Lutherans are notorious for enjoying the act of thinking. We Wesleyans are better known for our feelings and our busyness, our allegedly "warm hearts" and active hands rather than our clear heads and sound doctrines. Well, if you are thinking *that* about Methodist thinking, I intend to disabuse you of that thought. United Methodist theology is something quite beautiful in its own way—our special contribution to the liveliness of the body of Christ.

In our attempt to tie thought to practice ("practical theology"), our theological reflection on our spiritual pilgrimage ("the Scripture way of salvation") engenders a fresh theological perception of what it means to be a Christian. Our theological perception in turn encourages our implementation of Christian practices that are in keeping with that theology ("faith working through love"). All of our beliefs answer to a cardinal assertion of Wesley: "All learning without love is but splendid ignorance."

I'll admit that there have been times in the history of the Christian faith when concern for doctrine and theology have gotten in the way of discipleship: Let's all think about Jesus rather than follow him. Let's develop the Christian faith into a massive system that covers everything, that brings closure to all controversies and answers all questions.

In a sermon, Wesley excoriated those who were orthodox in their theology in a way that was deadly for their discipleship:

> . . . neither does religion consist in orthodoxy or right opinions; which, although they are not properly outward things, are not in the heart, but the understanding. A man may be orthodox at every point, he may not only espouse right opinions, but zealously defend them against all opposers; he may think justly concerning the incarnation of our Lord, concerning the ever blessed Trinity, and every other doctrine contained in the oracles of God. He may assent to all the three Creeds. . . . He may be almost as orthodox as the devil . . . and may all the while be as great a stranger as he to the religion of the heart.[3]

What Wesley is criticizing here is not orthodox theology but rather that deadly sort of theologizing that abstracts, distracts, and fossilizes the faith that ought to be a living relationship with the risen Christ. We are adept, you and I, at avoiding the claims of Christ, and sometimes a major means of avoidance is arguing about, dispassionately considering, and ruminating over Christ's claims. You will soon learn that if I am worried about Christian doctrine becoming a hindrance to Christian discipleship, it is very Methodist of me.

There was a time when some people characterized the thought of American Methodism as a rough-hewn, frontier theology for simple people. It was their explanation for why Methodism so successfully swept across the North American continent. Their contention was that Methodism reduced the gospel message to its threadbare, subjective essentials and traded in raw emotionalism in its backwoods revivals, making it easily accessible to simple folk on the frontier.

Most scholars now reject this simplistic description. Methodism succeeded in great part because it outthought, outpreached, and outserved some of its ecclesial competitors. Methodism, as it emerged here in America among the Methodists and the Evangelical United Brethren (the German-speaking Methodists), was a complex blend of elements from Puritanism, continental pietism, and Anglicanism, thoroughly rooted in the Reformation tradition but rephrasing that tradition in an innovative and challenging way that captured much of a young nation's religious imagination. There was a time when scholars of American religious history mined the writings and sermons of the Puritans to explain the major trajectory of American Christianity. Today there is a growing consensus among scholars that nineteenth-century Methodism may be the greatest contributor to the development of peculiarly American theological thought. If you want to understand contemporary evangelicalism, the peculiar way in which the Christian faith continues to grow and transmogrify in North America even as it rapidly declines in other Western democracies, and the relentlessly innovative and inventive nature of American Protestant Christianity, you are going to have to know something about how Methodists think.

United Methodist beliefs are those authoritative beliefs that are considered essential to who we are as Methodists and what we need to keep thinking if we are going to maintain our identity as Wesleyan Christians. I've heard people say, "What I like about being a Methodist is that you can believe fairly much whatever seems right to you." They are dead wrong, a scandal to the religious movement that is the lengthened shadow of John and Charles Wesley. Doctrinal indifferentism and theological latitudinarianism are perversions of our *Discipline*'s mandate for each of us to be active theologians.[4]

We stress the importance of our theological commitments when, by long-standing tradition, the bishop asks every candidate for the office of elder in full connection these questions:

> "Have you studied the doctrines of The United Methodist Church?"
> "After full examination, do you believe that our doctrines are in harmony with the Holy Scriptures?"
> "Will you preach and maintain them?"

If some perhaps well-meaning but intellectually slothful candidate were to respond with an inane "I think it doesn't matter so much what you believe as long as you are sincere," that candidate would promptly be dismissed by any self-respecting bishop on the grounds that "You seem to be a nice person but you are intellectually unfit to be a Methodist preacher."

We draw our doctrine from a number of sources. These are the texts that inform this book and, we are bold to believe, are gifts of God to the United Methodist Church to help us think about what God expects of us: Articles of Religion, Confession of Faith, *The Book of Discipline* (part 2), and *The United Methodist Hymnal* and *United Methodist Book of Worship.*

To be honest, in recent years United Methodist fights have mostly been over ethical issues rather than doctrines. Doctrinal indifferentism has been a malady among Methodists despite our Wesleyan origins. Perhaps if we focused more on doctrine we wouldn't have so many bitter, unproductive fights over ethics. Not a single ethical issue on which United Methodists seem willing to divorce one another is mentioned in the Apostles' Creed or the Articles of Religion. Go figure.

John Wesley praised theology that was "practical," that is, belief put into practice, belief in motion. Doctrine ought to be performed as sign of our faith in a Lord who invited and commanded, "Follow me." So consider these thoughts about United Methodist beliefs as equipment for discipleship, guides for the journey. These beliefs are what United Methodists think you need in order to walk with Jesus, a means of knowing that you are walking with the God whose name is Trinity rather than some godlet of your own sweet concoction. Our God did not come to us, we believe, in some vague, nondescript, and ethereal spiritual form. Our God came to us as a person with a face, with a name—Jesus the Christ. We cannot believe anything we please about the Trinity because of the incarnation (to mention two of our big beliefs). God became specific and, in love, came to us in the flesh, as Jesus of Nazareth. If we would think about this God, we must think about God specifically as Jesus the Christ, Son of God the Father, in the power of the Holy Spirit. We cannot use this God anyway we please. Our beliefs are ways that God uses us for God's purposes, stays close to us, forms us into a people who know how to worship the true and living God in all that we say and do.[5] We didn't think up this God (when we're creating "gods" of our own— otherwise known as idols—we always concoct deities more simple than the Trinity).

Here is an up-front warning about this book:

1. If you are one of those "it-doesn't-matter-what-you-believe-as-long-as-you-are-sincere" people, you may not like this book. Beliefs matter. Down through history people have committed all sorts of horrible acts, all the while sincerely believing that they were acting on the truth. Some beliefs are true and can be verified to a certain degree by methods that are appropriate to the truth that is asserted, and some beliefs are bogus, no matter how sincerely or widely they are held.

As a pastor I'm frustrated by folk who say, "I've lost my faith" as explanation for their noninvolvement in the church. Many of them mean "I lost the immature, unexamined faith that I picked up here and there in my childhood." I suspect that they are growing in faith rather than losing faith. Usually, the faith they lost is not the historic Christian faith. If you think that "having faith" means settling on a set of irrefutable propositions, bedding down and dozing through the rest of the sermon, this book may disturb you. I've had it with people who understand computer programming, French cooking, or molecular biology but assume that they can think like a Christian on the basis of simple, sappy truisms they picked up while flipping channels on their TV. The Gospels depict

Jesus as calling people to grow, not turn off their brains and settle into a life forever fixed at age seven.

What passes for atheism ("There is no God") or agnosticism ("I don't know whether or not there is a God") is sometimes simple cerebral sloth, intellectual sluggishness. Some people act as if their disbelief is an intellectual achievement when in reality it's a failure to think deeply about the Good News of Jesus Christ. The modern world is officially agnostic, contending that no truth is greater than any other truth, that it's fine to be a believer as long as you promise that your believing will never be more than a personal preference without political or economic implications. "I don't believe" sometimes means that disbelievers lack the intellectual chutzpa to think outside the box that the modern world has forced on them. We are a culture that loves shortcuts, slogans, facile definitions, and quick, easy, instant answers.[6] One of John Wesley's favorite biblical texts was "Work out your own faith with fear and trembling" (Phil. 2:12). Even though our salvation in Jesus Christ is free, it is not cheap. Jesus demands a lifetime of willingness to keep at the intellectual journey. In my eagerness to entice you, gentle reader, into the wonders of Wesleyanism, Lord help me if I make the gospel less demanding than it is.

2. If you're one of the "I'm-not-into-all-that-intellectual-theological-stuff" people, this book will be a reach for you. There is abroad the superficial notion that true spirituality takes us beyond the grubby particularities and limitations of all that dogma and doctrine to the "real thing," where all doctrines ultimately meet in some deeper, allegedly more inclusive realm of the spiritual. What this usually means is that we have only more successfully climbed deeper into our own subjectivity, thinking of our inner selves as the "real thing." Theology believes that the "real thing" is outside of us, the peculiar, particular God who has come to us in Jesus Christ to rescue us from our inner, detached, false selves.

Truth to tell, all of us are "theologians"—we talk about, think about, and listen for God. Everybody has a "theology," despite how uninformed and unformed. We are all under the heel of some "god" or another, whether we know it or not, including the "god" of our unformed subjectivity. Whenever something terrible happens to you and you say, "God, why did this happen to me?" or something fabulous happens to you and you say humbly, "God, why did this happen to me?" you are being theological. Just about everything we do, we do because we believe it. I began this morning by brushing my teeth, a practice that did not come naturally to me, a ritual that someone had to teach me as a child. Brushing my teeth arises from my "faith" that this practice can make a difference. Thus doctrine is not merely an expression of our beliefs but a means of forming us into different sorts of persons on the basis of our beliefs.

3. If you're one of those people who thinks that you are oh so much more clever than your great-grandparents, who believes that we are today privileged to stand at the summit of human development, then this book may sound awfully old. Chronological snobbery is endemic in modern people. As United Methodists, we try to believe what the saints before us believed. We are not the first to walk this way of discipleship. God has not left us to our own devices. Through Scripture and the church's historic confessions of faith, we have our imaginations stoked, fueled, and funded by those who lived considerably more interesting lives than we do. We go forward by looking backward. Ask a United Methodist, "Who are you?" and you'll likely get a story that starts at least with Wesley. Any faith that is merely contemporary is inevitably a shallow faith based only on that thin foundation of those who happen to be walking about right now. So in the church when we say, "I believe that . . . ," we are mostly talking history, affirming our membership in a community, saying, "The church has believed and I'm on my way to believing that. . . ."

4. And if you're one of those people who really believe the conventional "Religion is a private matter" or "I want to think for myself," you will be troubled by the authoritative tone of this book. One of the reasons that we come to church is to enable our beliefs to go public, to expose what we personally think to communal scrutiny and critique, to test our beliefs by exposing them to the judgments of Scripture and by subjecting them to the beliefs of our

sisters and brothers in Christ. All beliefs come from somewhere, are put in our minds by some external source; few beliefs simply arise from within our subjectivity. The person who says, "I feel more spiritual when I'm sitting at home watching Joel (or Rick, or Bob, or whomever) be religious than when I come to church" is right. Who doesn't feel vaguely content when you are alone and protected, secure in the prejudices that have been implanted in you simply by being a North American, capitalist, secular (all "beliefs" that you didn't come up with on your own) person? That's why this book is best read—like most Christian activity—in a group. Jesus saves us as a group, not merely as isolated individuals. One of the things Christians learn to fear most is that our thinking will be merely thinking for ourselves.

So you've been warned. And if, having been warned, you are still determined to forge ahead, I welcome you as a fellow traveler.

On the first Easter evening, a couple of disciples were trudging from Jerusalem toward the village of Emmaus (Luke 24:13–25). Suddenly, a stranger walked beside them. The stranger asks why they are so depressed. The two disciples are shocked that the stranger doesn't seem to know the terrible events in Jerusalem that crucifixion weekend. The stranger questions the disciples, then "opens the Scriptures." Still, the disciples don't understand. As evening falls, they invite the stranger to stay and have supper with them at an inn.

There, in the breaking of bread and the sharing of wine, their eyes are opened, and they see the stranger as none other than the risen Christ. The stranger vanishes, once again on the move. And the disciples run back to Jerusalem proclaiming, "We have seen the Lord."

This is a parable of Christian believing. We are on a journey. We believe some things about Jesus, but we don't understand everything. Through study of the Scriptures and conversation, we are questioned in our commitments. Not leaving us to our own devices, Jesus comes and walks with us, reveals himself, speaks, and gives us what we need to believe. Our lives are changed as we walk with him. We journey not alone. He is undeniably present to us, though still not completely grasped by us; he is on the move and never confined by us. And we run back home shouting, "We have seen the Lord."

That's sort of what we United Methodists mean when we say, "We believe. . . ."

William H. Willimon
Birmingham Area
The United Methodist Church
Lent 2007

1

We Believe in the Triune God

United Methodists profess the historic Christian faith in God, incarnate in Jesus Christ for our salvation and ever at work in human history in the Holy Spirit.[1]

"In the beginning when God . . ." (Gen. 1:1). That's the way the Bible begins. Our story starts with God. In fact, if God had not said, "Let there be . . ." we would have had no story to tell. We are conditioned by our culture to think that our life stories begin with us, with our initiative, our hard work, our own intellectual searching. We are heirs of the story that is modernity, the story that tells us that we are in control, gods unto ourselves. Knowledge is power. We think in order to gain control, to have power over ourselves and the world, to use the world and everyone in it for our egoistical ends. It is therefore somewhat of an offense to hear of a God whose love desires to control us for God's purposes, rather than the other way around.

The modern world teaches us that we are masters of our fate, captains of our souls. Rather than see ourselves as creatures, we like to think of ourselves as sovereign, free creators who construct ourselves through our astute choices and heroic decisions. What a shock to learn, through the testimony of Israel and the church, that the lives we are living may not be our own. As the psalmist puts it, "It is he who made us and not we ourselves" (Ps. 100:2). God made us before we had the opportunity to make up God.

The assertion that God makes us rather than that we make God flies in the face of what we have been taught about human thinking by modern cosmologists like Kant and Feuerbach. Immanuel

/ 1

Kant (1724–1804) put into our heads that the world is a chaotic, disorganized affair that assaults our senses with confusing phenomena. Our minds go to work on this mess of data and impose categories of space and time, arranging the world in a way that we find to be coherent and controllable.

See what's happened in Kant? The primal story of God creating and giving a good world in Genesis 1 has been exchanged for a counternarrative about our construction and constitution of a world that is better understood by us in order to be better controlled by us. The voice that now speaks, bringing something out of nothing, order out of chaos, and light out of darkness is no longer the voice of God (Gen. 1 and 2) but rather our own voices emanating from our own vaunted reason as we make a world to suit ourselves.

Although Kant cannot be wholly blamed for the way that modernity developed, it wasn't too great a leap from Kant's idea of a world that was rationally ordered by our minds working on the world to the atheistic humanism of Ludwig Feuerbach (1804–1872). Feuerbach, the progenitor of Freud and Marx, asserted that when we think we are talking about God we are merely talking about ourselves. Our ideas about God are "projections" of what we wish were true about God. What we call "theology" is just a screen on which we project collective human yearnings for the divine. Just as there's nothing really on a motion picture screen that is not put there by the projector, there is nothing factual about God, up there, out there, other than what we have projected through our own thoughts about God. "God" has no reality other than in our minds. It was not too great a step from Kant's notion of the world constructed by our minds to Feuerbach's "god" as a sometimes helpful, sometimes hurtful human construction. Having been made "in the image of God," as Genesis puts it, we returned the compliment.

Forgive me for boring you with Kant and Feuerbach. I do so only to remind you that when we think about God, we tend to do so within the limited confines of the modern worldview. So it is always a reach for people who live in a world like ours to think theologically, if by "theology" you mean thinking about God in a way that is fully open to the possibility that God may be a living, sovereign, free and active reality beyond the bounds of human construction and imagination.

The story that we are gods unto ourselves, autonomous, relatively powerful free agents—indeed, the only active agents in the world—is the story that holds us captive. We believe the lie that we are our own authors. This is the story that made possible many of the triumphs of the modern world and just about all of our truly great, bloody, contemporary tragedies. It is the officially sanctioned, governmentally subsidized story that makes our nation both powerful and violent, that makes many of us Americans so driven and so lonely, the story that has led to the ecological devastation of our planet and the plethora of false godlets who enslave and demand many of our lives.

To be a Christian means gradually, Sunday after Sunday, to be subsumed into another story, a different account of where we have come from and where we are going, a story that is called "gospel." You are properly called a "Christian" when it's obvious that the story told in Scripture is your story, above all other stories that the world tries to impose on you, and that the God who is rendered in Scripture is the God who has got you.

Christian Believing, A Work of God

It's important to begin by putting the matter of Christian believing in this way because if we don't, we might get confused into thinking that believing is something that we do—you must try very hard to believe all the things that Christians believe, you must lay aside your doubts and misgivings, your questions and your fears, close your eyes, clinch your fists, and believe.

No, we believe that if we are able to say, "I believe" that is a gift of God, something that God works in you, a result of what God as Father, Son, and Holy Spirit does among us, not our earnest intellectual achievement. If we say, as we Methodists regularly say in the words of the Apostles' Creed, "I believe in God the Father Almighty, . . . And in Jesus Christ his only Son our Lord; . . . I believe in the Holy Spirit . . ." we believe that's due to God's grace. No merely human being, limited by the boundaries of human thought and experience, can say anything of substance about God unless God first says something to us. That's why our beliefs begin neither in apologetic appeals to your reason ("Doesn't this make sense to you?"), nor by delving into the recesses of human experience ("Haven't you ever felt a special feeling? Well, that's God."), or by making some general assumptions about the nature of the world ("So beautiful and perfect a world must have been created by somebody wonderful. That's God."). We only know God from what God is willing to show us and say to us. So, in thinking about God, we've got to begin with God's self-revelation and self-disclosure, with God's talk to us about God. That's why we call Christianity a "revealed religion"—you couldn't have thought it up yourself.

Our heritage in doctrine and our present theological task focus upon a renewed grasp of the sovereignty of God and of God's love in Christ amid the continuing crises of human experience.

It comes as no surprise that United Methodists believe in God, though you may be challenged by what we believe about God, what God is up to, and what God expects of us. Note that we don't simply believe in "God"—some generic, pliable, vague deity. Sometimes you hear modern folk say something like "God? Oh, God is too grand, too large. We can't say anything for sure about God because God is a mystery."

We wish. What sounds at first like a humble, self-effacing statement—God is big and we are not, so we can't say anything for sure about God—can be another arrogant modern assertion. I refuse to receive what God wants to reveal to me in Scripture and the church; I refuse to be taught by anything beyond the bounds of my own limited human experience.

The Trinity

In saying, "We believe in God," we United Methodists are saying considerably more than just "We're not atheists." Like most Christians who are schooled in Scripture, we have no interest in the modern infatuation "Is there a God?" The Bible's question is "*Who is the God who is?*"

Our answer is the first of our beliefs and it is the same answer that is given by the majority of the world's Christians: We believe *in the triune God—Father, Son, and Holy Spirit.* The God who has come to us in Jesus Christ, the God who is portrayed in Scripture, is too gloriously complex, too undeniably active, to be indicated merely by a general concept, "God." We Wesleyans have therefore always taken care to point to *God's gracious self-involvement in the dramas of history* as a triune reality.

When you join our church, in the baptismal rite you are asked to make a Trinitarian confession of faith by using the Apostles' Creed. You are always baptized in the name of the Father, Son, and Holy Spirit. It's not too much of a stretch to say that being a Christian means to be someone who says, "I believe in the Trinity." With other orthodox Christians, we United Methodists are monotheists—we believe with Israel that God is one. Yet we are not *merely* monotheists. We haven't said, "God" until we've said, "Father, Son, and Holy Spirit." As John Wesley put it in his sermon on the Trinity, "These three are one." Although the word "Trinity" isn't a strictly biblical word, "Trinity" is a thoroughly consistent biblical name for the God who meets us everywhere in Scripture. In his *Notes on the New Testament*, Wesley finds the Trinity all over the place, standing behind the text, rising from it. In saying with Wesley that "these three are one," we are trying to talk about the complex biblical testimony that (1) God is the all-powerful Creator who is above and beyond us and our notions, and yet (2) Jesus, who lived among us, died and was raised by God, is also God; moreover, (3) the Holy Spirit, poured out on the church, as a personally powerful, palpably near presence among us is also God, and yet (4) God is one.

In his great sermon "On the Trinity," Wesley asserted that the doctrine of the Trinity "enters into the very heart of Christianity; it lies at the root of all vital religion,"[2] adding that it was the reality of the Trinity, in the work that the Trinity does among us, that was his chief concern, not some abstract philosophical speculation about the Trinity.[3]

In his Trinitarianism, Wesley put forth a dynamic, generous view of God. His stress on the Third Person of the Trinity, the Holy

Spirit, gave his theology a dynamic quality. Theologians speak of the "processional" work of the Trinity, the sending forth that goes on constantly in the divine nature. Indeed, I think that some of the Wesleyan stresses on a "sent" rather than "called" ministry—in which clergy are sent out to serve rather than called to fill a position—as well as Wesley's insistence that clergy be constantly on the move—itinerating from place to place—arise in great part out of Wesley's dynamic Trinitarianism. God—Father, Son, and Holy Spirit—constantly reaches out, moves toward us, proceeds into the "far country" (Luke 15) where we live. The word "apostolic" means simply "sent." It is the nature of this God to have a mission into God's world in which ordinary women and men are enlisted and sent forth to fulfill divine intent. Whenever that sending happens and people obey the commission of God to "Go! Tell!" then the church is truly "apostolic."

We are created to be in final, complete fellowship with this reaching, embracing God. Death is not oblivion but rather a move toward full communion with Father, Son, and Holy Spirit. Toward the end of Wesley's sermon on "The New Creation," Wesley links the Trinity to our eternal destiny—communion with God:

> And to crown all, there will be a deep, an intimate, an uninterrupted union with God; a constant communion with the Father and his Son Jesus Christ, through the Spirit; a continual enjoyment of the Three-One God, and of all the creatures in him![4]

Wesley's robust Trinitarianism put him at odds with prominent English intellectuals in the late seventeenth century. A gaggle of brilliant anti-Trinitarian thinkers like John Locke had launched an attack on the doctrines of the Incarnation and the Trinity. Thus was Deism born, a rather flaccid doctrine of God that many (albeit mostly unknowingly) hold today. Charles Wesley, brother of John, wrote a couple of hundred hymns (out of over two thousand!) in praise of the Trinity. Perhaps that is the best way to think about so complex a mystery—through poetry.

> By the Father, and the Son,
> And blessed Spirit made,
> God in Persons Three we own,

And hang upon his aid:
Reason asks, how can it be?
But who by simple faith embrace,
We shall know the mystery,
And see Him face to face.
(*Hymns on the Trinity*, #124)

We see in this stanza a tendency among us Wesleyans. While we moderately enjoy thinking about God, we would prefer even more also to experience and to enjoy God—to sing. The purpose of our thinking about something like the Trinity is "by simple faith," not simply to "know the mystery" but rather to "see Him face to face." We thus believe in God as a Trinity not only because we believe, with other Christians, that this is the only way adequately to talk about the God who is revealed in the Bible but also because we have experienced this multifaceted God in our lives.

So when we experience the living Christ, we experience nothing less than God with us in divine effulgence and lowliness at the same time, as Charles Wesley sings it:

Equal with God most high,
He laid his glory by:
He th'eternal God was born,
    Man with men he deigned t'appear,
Object of his creature's scorn,
    Pleased a servant's form to wear.
(*A Collection of Hymns*, #187)

The Trinity is the greatest intellectual achievement of the church, an attempt to come to terms with the reality of the Incarnation, that is, God with us, as one of us, in the flesh, incarnate in Jesus. God Almighty created the earth and all that is, hung the moon and stars and brought forth life where there had been nothing but chaos (Gen. 1).

Yet this God was born among us, walked where we walked, suffered as we must suffer, and died as we shall die. In his resurrection, Christ, though he was not with us as he had been in his earthly ministry, was undeniably present, in the bread and wine of Holy

Communion, in the preached word from Scripture, in the life of the church, prodding us relentlessly into the world, preaching and enacting the good news as the Holy Spirit. The earliest Christians came to the unanimous assertion that "God raised [Jesus Christ] from the dead" (Acts 13:30). Thus was Jesus—who taught us, walked among us, welcomed sinners, and partied with outcasts— vindicated as no less than God with us.

So any time we say, "we believe," we say in effect, "The Holy Spirit has come into our lives and shown us what we could never have seen on our own." Our belief, our insight, our faith is all the result of inspiration. Again, as Charles Wesley sang it,

> Spirit of faith, come down,
> Reveal the things of God,
> And make to us the Godhead known,
> And witness with the blood:
> 'Tis thine the blood to apply,
> And give us eyes to see,
> Who did for every sinner die
> Hath surely died for me.
>
> No [one] can truly say
> That Jesus is the Lord
> Unless thou take the veil away,
> And breathe the living word;
> Then, only then we feel
> Our interest in his blood,
> And cry with joy unspeakable,
> Thou art my Lord, my God!
>
> O that the world might know
> The all-atoning Lamb!
> Spirit of faith, descend, and show
> The virtue of his name;
> The grace which all may find,
> The saving power impart,
> And testify to all mankind,
> And speak in every heart!
>   (*United Methodist Hymnal,* #332)

Yet despite this three-fold complexity, God is one as Father, Son, and Holy Spirit.[5] As three candles exude one light, so the Trinity is mysteriously, gloriously one, said John Wesley.

You see this dynamic, generous Trinitarinism in the liturgies through which United Methodists worship God. For instance, "A Service of Word and Table 1" in the *United Methodist Hymnal* opens with a prayer that says we are able to speak to God only because of the "inspiration of your Holy Spirit," praying "in the name of Christ." The service proceeds into The Great Thanksgiving, which is divided into three main sections. The first thanks God the Father for creation and providential love. The second section gives thanks for Christ's life, death, and resurrection. The third invokes the Holy Spirit upon the bread and wine and upon the community. The prayer ends with "Through your Son Jesus Christ, with the Holy Spirit in your holy church, all honor and glory is yours, almighty Father, now and for ever, Amen."

Reduce the Trinity, and the Christian faith not only loses its complex way of talking about the active, energetic, resourceful God who is talked about in Scripture, but it is also in danger of truncating our experience of "God" into some vague, impersonal, indistinct, and therefore undemanding force who is inconsequential and unrelated to anything. We modern people tend to make God impersonal, abstract, and amorphous in order to render God innocuous and irrelevant. That way we can run the world as we please, safe in the rigidly enforced modern credo that "God is whatever you want God to be." The Trinity means that we are becoming who God wants us to be.

When there were some who wanted to take "In God we trust" off American money, others objected, saying, "We don't mean a Christian God, or God in the way Islam uses the word, just God however you want to think of God."

If that's all "God" means, why bother?

Neglect the Trinity, render us into mere monotheists, and the Christian faith is always in danger of becoming a set of beliefs, a philosophy of life, a helpful technique for getting what you want. This isn't orthodox Christianity.

But isn't this faith a set of beliefs? Isn't that what this book is about, United Methodist beliefs?

No. Christianity is first of all about the God who has come to us as a living, dynamic, complex personality who is Father, Son, and Holy Spirit. If we could adequately get this God fixed, defined, and stabilized into a set of beliefs, then the God we were believing in wouldn't be the God of the Bible, wouldn't be the living Lord. Therefore, United Methodists tend to stress faith in God as a relationship with a living, moving, demanding Lord rather than as a set of static ideas.

One of the main differences between a living God and a dead God is that a living God can still surprise you. In Trinitarian faith, it's not only that God once appeared, that God has spoken; it is also that God continues to reveal and to disclose, to appear and to show up when least expected or even wanted. God speaks. God continues to create something out of nothing, as in Genesis 1. And sometimes the something created out of nothing is a new you! If you can find a God who can be easily defined, pinned down with a creed, fixed by a set of absolute propositions, reduced to six fundamentals, go worship that. It will be easier than serving a God as loquacious, invasive, and demanding as the Trinity. But it won't be as much fun. It also won't be as true.

In talking about God in this fashion I am talking like an heir of John Wesley. In 1735, as Samuel Wesley lay dying, he called his son John to his bedside and urged him to seek a personal relationship with the living God through the Holy Spirit. Wesley later said that he had the form of faith without the personal experience of faith. Shortly thereafter, on his rough voyage to be a missionary in Georgia, John Wesley was deeply impressed by the Moravians on board whose firm faith challenged his own uncertainty. Back in England, Wesley met frequently with Peter Böhler, who stressed the pietistic religion of the heart.

Then, three days after his brother Charles had experienced a dramatic, heart-felt conversion, on Sunday, May 24, John Wesley's soul was engulfed by the living God:

> In the evening I went very unwillingly to a society in Aldersgate Street, where one was reading Luther's preface to the Epistle to

the Romans. About a quarter before nine, while he was describing the change which God works in the heart through faith in Christ, I felt my heart strangely warmed. I felt I did trust in Christ, Christ alone for salvation: And an assurance was given me that he had taken away *my* sins, even *mine,* and saved *me* from the law of sin and death.[6]

"Aldersgate" is a shorthand way of explaining why Methodism has always stressed the personal, relational, experiential reality of the triune God rather than some static, abstract divine set of attributes. It is of the nature of the Trinity—Father, Son, and Holy Spirit—to be in relationship, indeed to *be* relational in the deepest, most dynamic sense. To know, truly know, this God is to be in relationship with God, to have one's life engaged, engulfed, enflamed in a most assuredly personal way.

We believe God reaches out to the repentant believer in justifying grace with accepting and pardoning love. Wesleyan theology stresses that a decisive change in the human heart can and does occur under the prompting of grace and the guidance of the Holy Spirit.

To be sure, sometimes our stress on God in relationship with us, this Methodist "religion of the warmed heart," sounds to some like heart-happy pietists wallowing in our spiritual subjectivity, or anti-intellectual religion devoid of rational consideration. To those of us who follow in the procession of faith from the Wesleys, our response is that United Methodist stress on faith as an experienced, personal, engaging, and transforming relationship with God takes thinking to a deeper level and raises the bar on theological deliberation. Detached, abstract, cool consideration of God is not what theology is supposed to be. Rather, theology is thought determined by its Trinitarian object, the living God who has come out and grasped us in Jesus Christ and intends, in the power of the Holy Spirit, to change us.

Now, if what we United Methodists believe is true—that God as Father, Son, and Holy Spirit is always seeking relationship with us—then something else is happening as you read these poor words of mine. You will note in Scripture that just about anytime the story involves Jesus, something else is always happening. So

I'm thinking, as I've been rambling on, that the Trinity, whom I have been attempting to speak about, may be speaking to you, reaching out, creating something out of nothing, showing you things greater than what I could show you or you could see by yourself, enabling my awkward words to leap off the page and become almost like God's word addressed to you. That's why we United Methodists start by believing in God, a living, active God who is not only true but also busy, a God who reveals and discloses, refusing to abandon us to ourselves.

The best part of being a Christian is living with so interesting a God.

2

We Believe in Salvation through Jesus Christ

The created order is designed for the well-being of all creatures and as a place of human dwelling in covenant with God. As sinful creatures, however, we have broken that covenant, become estranged from God, wounded ourselves and one another, and wreaked havoc throughout the natural order. We stand in need of redemption.

We United Methodists have only recently gotten a reputation for having a rather rosy view of humanity. The longer Methodist view and the official positions of our church paint a different picture. Right at the beginning of our theological reflection, we admit that things are bad between us and God and between ourselves. When asked to list the absolutely essential beliefs of Methodists, John Wesley was remarkably brief: "(1) original sin, (2) justification by faith alone, (3) holiness of heart and life."[1] Note that Wesley begins with honest confession that we are, despite any of our good intentions, *sinners.*

How did we get the world, the way it is? Our beliefs as Christians don't tell us much about *how* the world got here; we leave that to the scientists. Yet we do believe that we know *why* there is something rather than nothing. "In the beginning when God created the heavens and the earth . . . God saw everything that he had made, and indeed, it was very good" (Gen. 1:1, 31). Our world is God's idea. All life is here for a good reason. We get an early glimpse of that purposeful creation in Genesis (the first book of the Bible, whose name means "Beginning"). "God said, 'Let us make humankind in our image' " (Gen. 1:26). While theologians argue

/ 13

over just to what "in our image" refers—reason, spirit, humor?—United Methodists state that purpose is "dwelling in covenant with God." There is something within the purposes of God that makes God invite us to join in God's work in the world. Thus the first humans, creatures though we are, are given a command to care for God's good garden that is the world and to "be fruitful and multiply," to propagate and to create in a way that we share some divine creativity with God.

Yet very early, at the dawn of our history with God, things go badly wrong. Not content to be creatures, we attempt to be gods unto ourselves, Promethian self-creators rather than creatures of the Creator. Discontent to be coworkers with God, we rebel, disobey, and take the world into our own hands. As soon as the primal couple produces children, one of the children becomes the first fratricide (Gen. 4) when Cain murders his brother Abel. Our bloodletting and head bashing is congenital.

We have broken that covenant, become estranged from God, wounded ourselves and one another, and wreaked havoc throughout the natural order. Read your morning newspaper, take Western History 101, visit your city dump, look within your own heart, and you will see we need not belabor or argue a major United Methodist belief: *We are sinners.*

Here's Wesley on our condition:

> We are already bound hand and foot by the chains of our own sins. These, considered with regard to ourselves, are chains of iron and fetters of brass. They are wounds wherewith the world, the flesh, and the devil, have gashed and mangled us all over. They are diseases that drink up our blood and spirits, that bring us down to the chambers of grace. But considered, as they are here, with regard to God, they are debts, immense and numberless. Well, therefore, seeing we have nothing to pay, may we cry unto him that he would "frankly forgive" us all.[2]

We did not turn out as God intended. "Prosperity theology" purveyed by popular TV preachers notwithstanding, we are not right. Having just crossed the threshold from perhaps the bloodiest, cruelest century ever into the terrorism and the wars against terrorism of our nascent century, well, we are not off to a particularly good future, are we? Still, all evidence to the contrary, some blithely assert that humanity is basically good, that we are all doing the best we can, and that down deep, we mean well and we are, when all is said and done, making progress. At first such optimistic assertions seem superficial and silly, and indeed they are. But then, a chief aspect of our sinfulness is to deny that we are, after all, down deep, *sinners*!

Wesley would call our superficial, power-of-positive-thinking sanguinity a result of the cardinal sin of pride. Again, gloomy, pessimistic (i.e., *truthful*) Father Wesley:

> From this evil fountain flow forth the bitter streams of vanity, thirst of praise, ambition, covetousness, the lust of the flesh, the lust of the eye, and the pride of life. From this arise anger, hatred, malice, revenge, envy, jealousy, evil surmisings: From this, all the foolish and hurtful lusts that now "pierce thee through with many sorrows," and, if not timely prevented, will at length drown thy soul in everlasting perdition.[3]

Jesus the Redeemer

Which then leads United Methodists to join with most of the world's Christians in admitting, ***We stand in need of redemption.*** Despite our alleged progress and our good intentions, we really do need saving. We can't seem to help ourselves by ourselves. We set out to do good and unintentionally cause great harm. We try to set the world right with our armies and our power only to cause a bigger mess. We say to one another, "I love you," when what we really mean is, "I love me and want to use you to love me even more." We habitually attempt to organize the whole world around ourselves, curving in on ourselves, living just for ourselves. We make firm declarations and resolutions and then throw them all away on a bottle of booze or a clutch of pills. We launch forth to make the world safe for democracy only to bomb and make mayhem among the very nations we presumed to save. Is it any wonder that, in an embarrassingly short time after creation of humanity, Genesis says sadly, "The Lord was sorry that he had made humankind on the earth and it grieved him to his heart" (Gen. 6:6)?

Our sin is not just private and personal but also systemic and social, political even. *We have . . . wounded ourselves and one another, and wreaked havoc throughout the natural order.* Paul says that the whole creation is groaning in travail (Rom. 8:22). That's a curious read on the world. In the modern world, when there is a hurricane or some other natural disaster, people ask, "Why did God do this to us?" Paul says that the whole creation groans as it asks humanity, "Why did you do this to God and God's world?"

The great English Catholic G. K. Chesterton was asked to submit an essay on the theme "What's Wrong with the Modern World?" Chesterton sent back a two-sentence article: "What's wrong with the world? *Me.*"

I know a bishop who urges his pastors to join with him in covenant to spend at least one hour a week with someone who is enslaved—to drugs, alcohol, sex, or success. This strikes me as a very Wesleyan spiritual discipline. Take out the Wesleyan bedrock belief that we are sinners, all the way down, that our sin is pervasive, relentless, and original, and the whole structure of Methodist believing collapses and Wesleyan sanctificationist theology is rendered into banal moralism. We don't want ever to lose sight of a primal fact: *We stand in need of redemption.*

And the Good News is that God did not give us what we deserve. Though God created us creatures to be in covenant and communion with our Creator, we grieved God by what we made of ourselves. Lonely and pitiful, all dressed up with our will-to-power and vain self-assertion, we were naked and forlorn in our rebellion. And just as the sky turned very dark and all seemed lost, God—true to God's Trinitarian nature—risked all, condescended, processed out, and embraced us. This is "gospel," the good news of Jesus the Christ.

We hold in common with all Christians a faith in the mystery of salvation in and through Jesus Christ.

Though "the Lord was sorry that he had made humankind" (Gen. 6:6), God preserved humanity from the devastating flood (Gen. 6) by the ark of Noah. And after the great flood, wonder of wonders, God makes a covenant, a promise to continue to work with and to love humanity (Gen. 9:8–10, 12–13). God, in a reckless act of love, pledges to stick with humanity no matter what. In response, all God asks of us is that we work with God in caring for the good creation (9:1–7). The story about God and us continues, by the gracious gift of God's covenanting with us.

Not that we kept our part of the bargain. What do you expect of a creature of whom it is said, "the inclination of the human heart is evil from youth" (Gen. 8:21)? God responds to our rebellion and disobedience with yet another covenant. On a starlit night God takes two childless senior citizens—Sarah and Abraham—and promises to make out of them a great family that shall be a blessing to all the families of the earth (Gen. 18). God has plans for them to be a "light to the nations." Thus Israel is born as a gracious act of a God who loves to bring something out of nothing and to make somebodies out of nobodies. All God asks of Israel, for its part of the bargain, is to worship "the Lord your God" in all its life together:

> You shall have no other gods before me. You shall not make for yourself an idol. . . . You shall not murder. You shall not commit adultery. You shall not steal. . . . (Exod. 20:2–4, 13–15)

Without boring you with the details (you can read Genesis through Malachi on your own) let's just say that, once again, things did not work out as God intended. It was Genesis 1–9 all over again. God gave us the law, the gracious gift of a God who refused to leave us to our own bumbling devices, a God who loved us enough to show us the way to life through the guidance of the law. God sent us the prophets, gracious gifts of a "long-suffering" God of "steadfast love." God gave us the priests and the Temple, means of propitiating for our sin. We disobeyed the law, we scorned the prophets, we abused the ceremonies of the Temple. Yet, as Paul said of God's covenant with Israel, "The gifts and the calling of God are irrevocable" (Rom. 11:29).

And so, in the "fullness of time" (John 1:16) the same God who made promises to us and who kept forgiving us when we broke our promises, the same God who kept coming back to Israel and resuming the conversation that we, by our sin had ended, this Holy and Righteous One lovingly moved in with the profane and the unrighteous. "The Word became flesh and lived among us" (John 1:14). We could not come to God, so God came to us. We could not, by our efforts, climb up to God, so God condescended to us. For United Methodist Christians, salvation has a face, a name, a particular way of living and dying, and rising and being present. That name is Jesus.

Through faith in Jesus Christ we are forgiven, reconciled to God, and transformed as people of the new covenant.

The Incarnate Christ

John Wesley often spoke of preaching as "offering Christ." For Wesley, preaching was more than a string of interesting ideas, even interesting ideas about Christ; it was experience of and engagement with Christ as a living, relational being. With other Christians we join in basing all that we say and know about God on the incarnation, the enfleshment of God in a Jew from Nazareth in whom we believe we have seen as much of God as we ever hope to see. Jesus is "the only Son from the Father" (John 1:14). He is not only the definitive revelation of God, but he is God, so much so that he was called "the Son of God." When the Creator said something decisive to creation, God said, "Jesus Christ," so much so that the Gospel of John calls Jesus "the Word," saying that "the Word was with God, and the Word was God" (John 1:1).

At the heart of the gospel of salvation is God's incarnation in Jesus of Nazareth.

All Christian theology, for certain all Wesleyan theology, is a series of implications and expositions on the primal, originating wonder that the Word was made flesh and moved in with us and we beheld in him the great glory of God. We believe that those dear folk who say—presuming intellectual humility—that God is ultimate, distant, ineffable, and unknowable, are wrong. God is not vague and indistinct, aloof and indiscernible. God has a face, a name, a certain way of talking and living, and dying, and rising. Jesus Christ—who lived briefly, died violently, and rose unexpectedly—is the One in whom "all the fullness of God chose to dwell" (Col. 1:19).

Let's be honest. When you listen, really listen to Jesus, as you get to know him as he is revealed in Scripture and present in the church in Word and sacrament, there is part of you that wishes that God had remained vague, indistinct, aloof, and indiscernible! What with Jesus' forgiveness of enemies, his nonresistance to evil, his denigration of the powerful, and his reaching out to the outcasts, well, Christians are those who are still getting over the shock that when God came and showed us the fullness of divine glory *it was Jesus!*

"Incarnation" is a word whereby we join other orthodox Christians in maintaining a difficult but saving truth: Jesus Christ was completely human and fully God. Jesus was not God in disguise, or a man who was almost divine; he was truly human, truly divine.

God came to us as a baby, born in a human family. Jesus hungered, thirsted, and hurt, just like us. He was tested and tempted like us (Heb. 4:15). He was no make-believe person, the final proof of which was his horrendous death on a cross. True, he was rightly human in a way none of us are. Though he was "tested as we are" says the Letter to the Hebrews, "yet he was without sin" (Heb. 4:15). Though we "walked in darkness" (Isa. 9:2), he was radiant light. Though we have this propensity to rebel against God and try to be gods unto ourselves, he was fully obedient, even obedient to death on a cross.

When we stand and affirm in the Apostles' Creed that he was "born of the Virgin Mary," we are telling the story that is incarnation. The "virgin birth" both claims Jesus' godly nature—he was not something that we worked for or thought up—and Jesus' human nature—he was born as we are born and died as we must die. The story of Jesus begins with a woman, an obedient woman who said in effect, "I don't know all that you are going to do for the world through me, but here I am, send me" (Luke 1–2). This is why the church traditionally spoke of Mary as the very first disciple. She was the first to hear the call of God in Christ and to say, "Yes."

The church got around to officially defining the incarnation at the Council of Chalcedon in 451. At Chalcedon we affirmed that although we say with monotheistic Israel "The Lord your God is one. . ." (Mark 1:29), now that we have been met by the Christ, we can never be mere monotheists. Yet we are not tritheists either. At Chalcedon, we tried to say what we had witnessed of God in Christ, reconciling the world. Jesus Christ was not a subordinate extension of God, or a second sort of God; Jesus Christ was

> the only Son of God,
> eternally begotten of the Father,
> God from God, Light from Light,
> true God from true God,
> . . . .
> of one Being with the Father;
> through him all things were made,
> For us and for our salvation
> he came down from heaven,
> . . . .
> (*United Methodist Hymnal,* #880)

It's tough being Trinitarians who worship God Incarnate in a world that loves simplistic solutions and monistic principles. We wouldn't even try were it not that, having been met by Jesus Christ, we can no longer think about God in simple ways. Thus we can have sympathy with the dear soul who says, "Hey, we have our doctrinal differences, but down deep, aren't all religions about the same? We all worship the same God, right?"

Wrong. Just when we were all set to worship a God who seemed distant, indistinct, therefore undemanding and irrelevant, a God who could be utilized in our pet causes and to fulfill our assumed needs, we met God in the flesh, Jesus the Christ. He managed to be both very close to us, very much like us, and absolutely distant from us, very unlike us. He both stood next to us in our suffering and walked on ahead of us in our complacency. So if you are aggravated with Christians in general for talking in such seemingly convoluted and complex ways, and with United Methodists in particular, please know that we are trying to think about the almost unthinkable—"In Christ, God was reconciling the world to himself" (2 Cor. 5:19).

Scripture witnesses to the redeeming love of God in Jesus' life

and teachings, his atoning death, his resurrection, his sovereign presence in history, his triumph over the powers of evil and death, and his promised return. Because God truly loves us in spite of our willful sin, God judges us, summons us to repentance, pardons us, receives us by that grace given to us in Jesus Christ, and gives us hope of life eternal.

Atonement

The way Scripture tells the story—and we would know nothing about Jesus without Scripture, for here is a story so wonderfully strange we could have never thought it up ourselves—Jesus is not only God with us but God actively doing something about the problem that exists between us and God. We call that divine work in Christ and on his cross "atonement"—at-one-ment. The atonement names that dramatic process of divine love through which God did something decisive in Jesus Christ about the separation between us and God. Note, in the above thickly packed quote from our *Discipline* that Jesus' work is described as "redeeming," "atoning," work that is "triumph" as well as that which "judges" us, "summons . . . ," pardons us, receives us," and "gives" us. God doesn't just sit back, saying, "You know, don't you, how much I love you?"

God acts, moves, works, triumphs, gives, and forgives. I note this because it is my impression that many Americans have had our theological imaginations truncated with a flaccid deism that renders God into an allegedly compassionate but essentially inactive and uninvolved sort of deity. Deism says that while God may have created the world, God fairly quickly retired and has left us to ourselves.

As we have noted, deism always sent Wesley into orbit. Wesley not only thought that without the Trinity we cannot follow God, but that without the self-revelation of God in Christ and the work of the Holy Spirit we can know nothing of God. Walk all you want in the woods, hug a tree, or listen to the song of a bird, but you will still not know much about God. In 1757 Wesley wrote a lengthy polemic against Bishop Taylor's deistic claim that "heathens" (i.e., those who lack the revelation of God in Christ) have sufficient knowledge and power to know God and obey God's will. No, said Wesley. Only God can reveal God.

Against deism of any stripe, United Methodists believe God is very, very busy. The name for God's busyness among us in Christ and the Holy Spirit is *atonement*. Jesus' life, death, and resurrection demonstrate that any God who would reach out in love to the likes of us has got to be a God who doesn't shrink from much blood, sacrifice, and death, for we are murderous toward our would-be saviors. To redeem us, a high cost must be paid. Jesus risked all and got down and dirty with us sinners in order to embrace us and carry us home. He atoned and redeemed.

Who was Jesus? Jesus was a wonderful teacher and preacher. Many found in his teaching, words that wisely pointed the way to greater love of God and neighbor. However, when some sincerely tried to follow the way that was cast by this great teacher, they found it virtually impossible. It would have been one thing if the teacher had urged us simply, "Do not worry about tomorrow" (Matt. 6:34), which might have led us to greater peace of mind. But he went on to say that we should love our enemies (Luke 6:35), pray for rather than revenge our enemies (Matt. 5:44), and hate our mothers (Luke 14:26). Such talk forever disturbed our peace. Paul spoke for us all: "I do not do the good that I want, but the evil I do not want is what I do" (Rom. 7:19). That many believe that Christianity is mostly about "trying to live a good life and being kind to your neighbor" suggests that they have never actually listened to or tried to practice the teachings of Jesus!

Who was Jesus? He was not just a great ethical teacher; he was the Redeemer who went to the cross and "died for our sins," as the church said from the first, attempting to account for the significance of Jesus' death on the cross. We are, as we have admitted, sinners. Whatever is to be done about us can't be done by us. Our debts are too great, our lives too corrupt and deformed. So somehow, in the cross of Christ, God took up our sin, our propensity to serve death rather than life, and redeemed us (bought us back from slavery to sin and death), atoned for us (did something about the great gap between us and God), judged us (our sin is deadly serious), and pardons us (writes off our debts that we have incurred through sin).

Note that the *Discipline* doesn't spend much verbiage in attempting to explain just how this happens. For us, God's reconciling the world in Christ is a great mystery that we Wesleyans would rather experience and live into rather than explain. All we know is that, from the testimony of Scripture and in our own experience, God in Christ did something decisive at Calvary, wrought a victory that totally rearranged relations between God and humanity.

> Whoever wishes to become great among you must be your servant, and whoever wishes to be first among you must be slave of all. For the Son of Man came not to be served but to serve, and to give his life a ransom for many. (Mark 10:43–45)

Yet even to say this is, for us Wesleyans, not to say enough about Christ. Calvary is not the end of our story with God, but its true beginning. In cross and resurrection, Christ did not simply say to us, "You're saved. Go in peace and one day enjoy your time in heaven." In his resurrection, Jesus was not only raised from the dead, but he also came back to life with us. He came back *to us* telling us not only, "Because I live you shall live also" but also calling us to live *for him.* He came back to the very folk who had so disappointed and betrayed him in his death and recalled them to "follow me." He gave his disciples work to do—his work—and life to live—his life—and truth to tell—his truth. In other words, he came back to us and once again covenanted with us, promised to be with us until the "end of the age" (Matt. 28:20), then told us, "Go! Make disciples of all nations. . . ."

Jesus Christ is the singular way to friendship with God for all people. His way is not easily meshed with other ways or salvations. To be sure, it is possible to encounter God outside Christianity, yet when one does, we believe that one is encountering the God who is Jesus the Christ, in the power of the Holy Spirit, whether one knows it or not. Anytime anyone anywhere is truly met by the true and living God, we believe this meeting is in the light of Jesus Christ, the one of whom it can be truthfully said, "In him was life, and the life was the light of all people" (John 1:4). Salvation is uniquely tied to this Jew from Nazareth. In saying that Jesus Christ is the final, unique way to God we are only saying what Scripture says repeatedly. We do not claim this about Jesus in order to put down other religions but to lift up the way of Jesus. We have no need to prove other religions false but rather joyously to live Christianity as true.

There's something about this God that just won't stop trying to make something out of us, even after we killed God's only Son. Thus we call it the New Testament, the new covenant that Christ not only makes with us but enables us to keep. Whereas many Christians, both Protestant and Catholic, have emphasized a juridical view of the Christian life—Christ atoned for our sins and by his sacrifice paid our debt to God—Wesley, while not rejecting the juridical, had a more therapeutic view of Christian life. The atonement wrought by God enables us to grow in God, daily to overcome and to be healed of some of the sin in which we have been bound.

Who *is* Jesus? He is the One who has come among us in order to help us in our weakness. God is personal, a person, who relates to persons. On his cross, Jesus was excruciatingly (no pun intended) present, in solidarity with us. In this sense, atonement and incarnation are much the same thing. What happened at Calvary was begun at Bethlehem. Eternity touched time in Jesus. He came among us and modeled for us what it meant to be a servant of God and today enables us to be servants of God.

Jesus didn't just talk about heaven as a place somewhere, someday; he spoke of "the kingdom of heaven." The word "kingdom" is political, implying boundaries and demarcation. It is not some subjective feeling inside us but a present, observable fact outside us that challenges the kingdoms of this world. So Jesus' challenge wasn't simply the intellectual "Do you agree?" but the more engaging, political, and decisive "Will you join up?"

So when they asked Jesus if he was really the Messiah (that is, the sign and the inauguration of God's promised reign), he pointed to the "political" results of his work:

The blind receive their sight, the lame walk, the lepers are cleansed, the deaf hear, the dead are raised, and the poor have good news brought to them. (Matt. 11:5)

Love, Urging Us On

Furthermore, Jesus is not just someone who did something beneficial for us two thousand years ago but also someone who is raised from the dead, present with us, nearer to us than we are to ourselves. Thus Paul made statements like "The love of Christ urges us on" (1 Cor. 5:14) and "It is not I, but Christ who lives in me" (Gal. 2:20). So after Easter it's not right to speak of Jesus in the past tense ("Christ was . . ."), or even in the future tense ("Christ will be . . ."), but to discipline our speech to the present "Christ *is.* . . ." Having the love of Christ among us and in us, all of us are called to active participation in his ministry, speaking the same way he spoke, walking the same way he walked, loving the same way he loved.

From the Wesleys we get a rich sense of the complexity of the living Christ, his various "offices" (as the church has termed the different aspects of Christ's activity in our behalf) of prophet, priest, and king. Note these three stanzas of a Charles Wesley hymn:

> 6 Prophet, to me reveal
>   Thy Father's perfect will:
>   Never mortal spake like thee,
>   Saviour, who shall pluck me thence?
>   Faith supports, by faith I stand,
>   Strong as thy omnipotence.
> 7 On thee my Priest I call,
>   Thy blood atoned for all:
>   Still the Lamb as slain appears,
>   Still thou stand'st before the throne,
>   Ever off'ring up my prayers,
>   These presenting with thy own.
> 8 Jesus, thou art my King,
>   From thee my strength I bring:

Shadowed by thy mighty hand.
Saviour, who shall pluck me thence?
Faith supports, by faith I stand,
Strong as thy omnipotence.
Shadowed by thy mighty hand,
Shadowed by thy mighty hand.
("Hymn to the Son," #186)

Scripture teaches us that Christ was/is a "prophet." In the Bible, a prophet is not so much someone who foretells the future as someone who "forthtells" the truth of God. Prophets tell the truth. And because we're who we are, prophets are usually persecuted and rejected. In Luke 4, when Jesus read and quoted from Scripture, the congregation's admiration quickly turned to wrath. Jesus is prophet not only in that he tells us the truth, whether it hurts or not, but he said, "I am the truth" (John 14:6). Here is truth in bodily form.

> The Spirit of the Lord is upon me, because he has anointed me to bring good news to the poor. He has sent me to proclaim release to the captives and recovery of sight to the blind, to let the oppressed go free, to proclaim the year of the Lord's favor. (Luke 4:18–19)

Jesus was crucified not only as a sacrificial victim to save us from our sin but also because he told the truth and enacted the truth before a bunch of sinners like us, and we, sinners that we are, responded the way we always respond to unpleasant, unwanted truth: with violence.

Jesus was/is a "priest." The Letter to the Hebrews notes that in the Temple priests offered sacrifices to God to atone for our sin. They managed and mediated dealings between God and humanity. So it is quite understandable that Christians came early to believe that Christ was a priestly sacrifice for the sins of all. Jesus' blood shed on the cross somehow did something about our terrible sin. When John the Baptist saw him, he called Jesus "the lamb of God who takes away the sins of the world" (John 1:19), the same song that we sing when we celebrate Holy Communion today. Our sin is serious and any attempt by God to do something about the gulf between us and God will involve serious work on God's part.

This is what Christians mean when we say, "Christ died for our sins." Christ did for us, on the cross, which we could not do for ourselves—made atonement in our behalf. In Jesus, God the Father received a gift from God the Son, and God the Son embodied and enacted the resourceful, relentlessly seeking love of God the Father. Thus we see on the cross, and in all the work of Jesus, the truth in Jesus' most famous parable, the Prodigal Son. When criticized because he fraternized with, ate and drank with sinners, Jesus responded by telling this story of a young man who insulted and forsook his father and when, in rags and ruin, turned his steps toward home:

> While he was still far off, his father saw him and was filled with compassion; he ran and put his arms around him and kissed him. (Luke 15:20)

Jesus is the definitive statement that there is something in God that is determined to seek and to save, to win back and to make right, the lost.

Jesus Christ was/is the royal one. He was greeted by little children when he entered Jerusalem as "Son of David," that is, in the lineage of Israel's greatest king. And when he died, they put a sign over his wounded head that read, "King of the Jews." His resurrection, in which he royally triumphed over sin and death, was a royal victory.

So it's not enough to say simply that "Jesus was a great moral example" or "a fine teacher of truth." He is Lord. He has been raised in order to rule. He sits "at the right hand of God the Father Almighty" as we say in the creed. Therefore it is not enough to think of the Christian faith as something personal and private. It is that, but it is more. This thing between us and God is cosmic, large, political, social, a new heaven and a new earth. To say, "I believe in Jesus Christ" is to make a grand political claim. It is to assert, sometimes all present evidence to the contrary, that we know who sits on the throne, who is in charge, who will write the last chapter of the story between us and God, and who will right the wrong that we've done in the world. He shall rule.

Paul says that Jesus was

> Raised from the dead. . . . He disarmed the rulers and authorities and made a public example of them, triumphing over them in it. (Col. 2:12, 15)

Connecting Christ's militancy with his royalty, Paul says to the Ephesians:

> God put this power to work in Christ when he raised him from the dead and seated him at his right hand in the heavenly places, far above all rule and authority and power and dominion, and above every name that is named, not only in this age but also in the age to come. (Eph. 1:20–21)

Please remember this political, militant talk from Scripture the next time you hear someone complain—as you are bound to hear—that we United Methodists mix religion and politics, and take public, sometimes controversial stands on political issues. We really believe Jesus Christ is Lord—of all.

Jesus was/is the resurrected one. The resurrection was not simply a matter that Jesus was raised from the dead, not even a matter that one day, through him, we shall all have eternal life in heaven, though all that is implied. The resurrection was God's dramatic vindication of Jesus. If you have ever wondered, "What does God look like?" or "Whose side is God on anyway?" then the resurrection is God's definitive answer. God vindicates the path of suffering, obedient love. God refuses to win victories through violence. God is on the side of forgiveness and peace. So whenever Christians are asked, "Who is the God you worship?" we can respond that (in the words of Lutheran theologian Robert Jenson), "God is whoever raised Jesus Christ from the dead."

And when we Christians ponder our future with God, we believe that, through an amazing act of grace, the same God who raised Jesus from the dead shall bring us along as well. The same God who sought us and suffered for us all the way to death shall not forsake us in our deaths. "Christ was raised from the dead, the first fruits of those who have died. . . . Death has been swallowed up in victory. . . . Thanks be to God, who gives us the victory through our Lord Jesus Christ (1 Cor. 15:20, 54, 57).

We come back to the beginning. John begins his Gospel with "In the beginning was the Word" (John 1:1). The Word, the eternal Logos, the Christ, was with God at the beginning and was God. Although through human sin things did not go with the world as God intended at the beginning, now Christ, "the Word made flesh," is finishing what God began; God is at last getting God's way with the world.

In this Jew from Nazareth, God is getting what God wants. We are his new creations. "For in him all things in heaven and on earth were created, things visible and invisible, whether thrones or dominions or rulers or powers—all things have been created through him and for him" (Col. 1:16).

3

We Believe in the Holy Spirit

We share the Christian belief that God's redemptive love is realized in human life by the activity of the Holy Spirit, both in personal experience and in the community of believers.

If you are reading this book about United Methodist Christian beliefs, and if you are getting anything out of it, it's not primarily because I'm a good writer or you are an astute reader. It is happening as a gift of grace. And the power of gift, in this faith, the engine driving faith itself, has a name—the Holy Spirit. If ever Christians say something like "I am saved," we mean it in the passive, present, and future tense. Our salvation is a work of God in us—then, on the cross; now, in our daily walk with Christ; and into the future God has for us. That work by God has a name—the Holy Spirit. As it is the self-assumed task of God in Christ to speak to us, to show us the way, to receive our sins, to intercede for us, to die for us, and to rise for us; it is the work of God in the Holy Spirit to initiate faith in us, to nurture faith, and to bring faith to its full fruition, to "perfect us in love," as Wesleyans like to put the matter. The Holy Spirit is God perfecting what God begins in us, through the Holy Spirit, and what God shall finally bring to complete fruition and consummation in us, in the Holy Spirit.

It's one thing to say that you believe that there is a God; it's quite another to believe that God is there for you. There are too many reasons, reasons having to do with who we are (sinners) and who God is (holy, righteous) that we cannot come to God on our own. We must be brought to God by God. (In a parable, Jesus said that the good shepherd sought the lost sheep, and when he found it, he put the sheep on his shoulders and brought the sheep back home. Jesus shows little interest in what the sheep thought of the whole affair.) Salvation is God's having sought and saved the lost and brought them home. The Holy Spirit makes that possible. With all Trinitarians, we live in Christ, by the power of the Holy Spirit, to the glory of God the Father. So having spoken of Christ, God the Son, we move immediately to speak of that means by which we are given saving knowledge of and saving ability to follow Christ:

. . . the activity of the Holy Spirit, both in personal experience and in the community of believers. This community is the church, which the Spirit has brought into existence for the healing of the nations.

What Jesus did for us on the cross is "realized in human life" (to use the words of the *Discipline*) through the Holy Spirit for the whole world. What God said to us, God says to us, in Scripture, now, effectively and engagingly through the Holy Spirit. The Bible is an ancient book, written in languages quite unlike our own, in a culture unlike our own. Furthermore the Bible is a book of truth, the truth which is Jesus Christ, whereas we mostly enjoy books that deceive us about the real truth about ourselves.

How can modern, limited sinners like us say, "That passage of Scripture really spoke to me"? We could not, except for the illuminating, enlightening work of the Holy Spirit in us. John Wesley believed that Scripture is "God breathed." That is, Scripture is "inspired" (literally, filled with Spirit, breathed) by God, in its inception by God and its reception by us. We mean this when we have traditionally said that the Holy Spirit "illumines" or "enlightens" us.

A persistent charge against eighteenth-century Methodism was "enthusiasm." (In Christian theology "enthusiasts" are those who hear God speaking directly—who rely on this direct experience of God, without checking their direct perception of God by means of the Scripture, the history of Christian thought, the traditions and decisions of the church, the dictates of reason, or much else.) Wesley's writings contain more than two hundred references to enthusiasm, mostly as Wesley's defense against the charge, but some of them are his grateful acceptance of the label "enthusiast" in the face of his more staid critics. Wesley deeply believed that God routinely and quite dramatically intervened in the world to push forward God's purposes and to defend and protect God's saints, and he joyfully ascribed all sorts of events in his life and in the life of early Methodism to the intervention of the Holy Spirit.

God at Work in Us, for Us

Because the Holy Spirit is a member of the Trinity—that is, God—the Holy Spirit enables us truly to encounter Christ in our reading of Scripture. The Holy Spirit produces Scripture, enlightens our reading and hearing of Scripture, and enables us to perform Scripture. Miraculously, when we read Scripture, Christ stands among us, present through our reading and hearing of mere words. There is no way that we could accomplish such a feat on our own. You may have noted that when we United Methodists read Scripture on Sunday morning, we usually precede the reading with a Prayer for Illumination, such as the following:

> Lord, open our hearts and minds by the power of your Holy Spirit so that, as the word is read and proclaimed we might hear your word for us today. Amen.

The Holy Spirit helps us in our weakness, says Paul.

As we Methodists say, this presence of Christ's love through the testimony of the Holy Spirit is *both in personal experience and in the community of believers.* The Holy Spirit's work evokes deep feelings in us as individuals—those wonderful moments when, while listening to a sermon or reading Scripture, we say, "I get it!"—and it is also a communal, corporate phenomenon. In a pivotal passage in the Acts of the Apostles, chapter 2, the Holy Spirit descends like fire upon a whole group of apostles, forming these strangers into the church. Something there is about this Spirit that gathers a crowd, overleaping barriers of race, language, gender, and class to make a new people. Thus when we speak of baptism, we say that we are made Christians "by water and the Spirit." The Holy Spirit forms the church out of nothing, not as most human communities are formed—through affinities of class, self-interest, or economic location—but rather by the work of the Holy Spirit, just as the Spirit hovered over the dark waters at creation and brought forth a world out of nothing.

The church is therefore that human gathering that wouldn't be here, and certainly could never survive, without the creative, convening work of the Holy Spirit. If you are here, in the church, reading this book, trying to be a better follower of Jesus, we believe it's because the Holy Spirit put you here. You think you bought this book because you wanted it! Well, perhaps you sort of wanted it, but I believe that if you bought this book on United Methodist beliefs and have made it thus far, it is testimony to the enlightening, prodding wind of the Holy Spirit breezing through your life.

It does seem to us United Methodists that it is of the nature of the Holy Spirit to provoke and to enable change. The Bible speaks about change most often through the word "repentance"—to turn around, to be transformed, to move from one mode of life to another, to be more of the person that God intended you to be, to turn from sin and to turn toward God. Such turning we consider to be (are you surprised?) a work of God in us through the persistence of the Holy Spirit. So, on the day of Pentecost, when Peter is asked by the crowd, "What must we do?" he replies, "Repent and be baptized in the name of Jesus Christ, so that you may have your sins forgiven and receive the gift of the Holy Spirit" (Acts 2:38).

Repentance—turning from ourselves and turning toward God—we Wesleyans believe to be a lifetime process. We never get so adept at worshiping and serving God that we no longer need to repent. Daily, said Jesus, we are to take up our cross and follow. And daily we are to let go of the crushing burdens the world puts on our shoulders so that we might take up the burdens Jesus has in mind for us. Sin is so deeply rooted in our thinking and willing that only a lifetime of God's work in us can root it out. The Good News is that through the work of the Holy Spirit, we keep turning. God isn't done with us yet.

The church ought to be that sort of community whose work is

so risky, whose mission is so bold, and whose success is so unimaginable that the church will fail utterly unless the Holy Spirit empowers it to be that which God calls the church to be. Jesus said that if we work for him, they will drag us before law courts and judges, kings and cops, but we need not fear. The Holy Spirit will tell us what to say (Luke 21:12).[1]

The Transforming Power of God

I fear that sometimes the church has meetings; builds great-big, heavy buildings; and makes long lists of rules in a desperate effort to be the church without being dependent on the Holy Spirit to be the church. The tasks undertaken by the church ought to be those tasks that, if accomplished, can only be ascribed to the Holy Spirit. So the other day, when we raised enough money to make our annual church budget, despite a rise in the budget and a bad economic climate, someone said, "It's a miracle!" That was an everyday acknowledgment that God is miraculously active here, now. We have been taught to name that eventful activity "Holy Spirit."

A strong faith in the reality and resourcefulness of the Holy Spirit (what theologians call "pneumatology"—*pneuma,* Greek for "wind" that is also rendered "spirit" or "breath" in the New Testament) accounts for why United Methodists have not been into biblical fundamentalism. We have too much respect for the thickness and largeness of Scripture to reduce the bubbling vitality of the Bible to a set of "fundamentals" and too much respect for our own sinfulness to think that we've got the truth by the tail. More than that, we are deeply convinced that Scripture is the playground of the Holy Spirit. Scripture is always more than the letter that is fixed and stolid, arms folded and scowling at us from the page. Scripture is—by the grace of the Holy Spirit—a lively, speaking presence among us, prodding us, summoning us, pulling us toward God. No "fundamentals," no matter how long a list we could come up with, can do that.

At our best, we link pneumatology and ecclesiology. Whereas when Roman Catholics tend to stress the church as an institution united by its bishops, Wesleyans tend to see the church as a pneumatological phenomenon, a miraculous creation, ever fresh in each new time and place by the Holy Spirit. Sometimes there is a tension between the work of the lively Holy Spirit and the often-deadening reality of the institutional church. Our church is never half as lively as the Spirit that gave us birth.

Our Wesleyan pneumatology accounts for why United Methodists find ourselves on the forefront of certain social changes and transformative movements. We have always been active in peace movements, the civil rights movement, the women's movement, the early labor movement, and the child welfare movement. And we were among the first to ordain women to full leadership in our churches. We ordained women not because we thought that women had the "right" to be ordained, though that is true, but rather because we really believed that leadership is a gift to the church by the Holy Spirit. And as Jesus said, "The *pneuma* blows where it will" (John 3:8).

Any time in our history when we have settled down to keep house as we are, just us and our good friends, content to put down roots, settle in, fixed and established at this one time and place, then that good-old prodding, pushing Holy Spirit blows through our settled arrangements, rips us up, moves us forward and we—kicking and screaming or dancing and parading—move forward. Many of the Pentecostal churches born in the last century, sweeping like wildfire across the world today, have their roots in Methodism. Pentecostalism may be one of Methodism's greatest gifts to the universal church. South American liberation theologian José Miguez Bonino calls Wesley a grandfather in the faith. I believe that our expansive pneumatology accounts for why about 75 percent of the Wesleyans in the world and about 20 percent of the United Methodists in the world are beyond the bounds of the United States. The Holy Spirit blows where it will.

Scripture depicts the Holy Spirit as having certain recognizable, consistent tendencies—like comfort and compassion. As Jesus prepares to leave his disciples, he tells them that he will not leave them alone. He will send to them an "Advocate," who will be with them and will now speak to them about God and will speak for them to God (John 14:16). When Philip, one of the first to lead the church, is pushed out into the desert, there to meet a man from an exotic, foreign land—a man of another race and sexual disposition—the man asks to be baptized, to join Jesus' family, and Philip does just that. When Philip gets back to Jerusalem, the church wants to know how on earth Philip felt authorized to do such a radically inclusive act. Philip's defense: the Holy Spirit made me do it; I would have never thought up something so courageous, outlandish, or loving on my own (Acts 8:26–40).

And when Peter and a group of his fellow Jews gathered at Pentecost, and the house shook as if in an earthquake, and everyone began to talk funny and to hear funny, there was such a ruckus that a crowd outside in the street sneered, "They are drunk!" Peter came out to the street and said, in effect, "We're not drunk with spirits, though we are filled with the Spirit. The prophets of old foretold a day when God's Holy Spirit would empower everybody to be a prophet—young and old, maids and janitors, high and low. That day is now!" (Acts 2:1–41). The creative Holy Spirit didn't stop creating something out of nothing when the world was done; the creativity continues and new worlds keep coming into being, all by the work of the Holy Spirit.

How typical of United Methodists not to leave it at that. We believe that the Holy Spirit is not our possession, to be used to make our lives a bit more meaningful. Americans tend to be utilitarians about everything, even God. The elusive, uncontrollable, and uncontainable Holy Spirit is what God uses to work in us rather than what we use to get a grip on God. When we Wesleyans are accused of being too busy, too active in working for the kingdom, we blame our sometimes frenetic industriousness on the prodding of that relentless Holy Spirit. Jesus is rarely presented in the Gospels as static and at rest. He is no office-bound bureaucrat, posting office hours and waiting for us to call; he is the seeking shepherd, the searching woman, the intruding prophet, the busy farmer. God will have us. That divine determination is a work of the Holy Spirit.

So in United Methodist lore we all know the story of John Wesley, priggish little Oxford don who ran hither and thither, working, praying, studying, traveling as a would-be missionary to the heathens in Georgia, only to be blindsided by God's reassuring grace while at (of all places) a church meeting on Aldersgate Street in London on May 24, 1738. There, quite apart from all that Wesley had been doing for God, the Holy Spirit did something to Wesley. John Wesley wrote that his heart was "strangely warmed," not by just any heart-warming sentiment but rather by the following assurance: "I did trust in Christ, Christ alone, for salvation . . . that Christ had taken away *my* sins, even *mine*, and had saved *me* from the law of sin and death."

His statement about Aldersgate from his *Journal* is clearly, classically Protestant: justification (pardon, forgiveness) of sinful humanity by the work of Jesus on the cross and resurrection. The new stress that Wesley now gave to such classical belief was its appropriation in the life of the believer, the experience of assurance of that justification (the "witness of the Spirit" as he called it). And this is why Wesleyans tend to stress the delightfulness and the necessity of "heartwarming" experiences of God's love—conversion, regeneration, being born again—as pneumatological gifts of a most-determined Holy Spirit.

As we recall Wesley's "heartwarming" experience we do well to remember that we are thinking about Wesley's encounter in a culture in which personal, emotional, subjective experience is more important than just about anything, including God. When we say, "I believe . . ." we rarely mean, "I affirm the historic teachings of the church" or "I believe in the truthful authority of Scripture." What we usually mean by "I believe" is "It seems personally right to me that. . . ." We judge every assertion of truth on the basis of personal experience, truth as a matter of individual perspective— "Well, you see it your way; I see it my way; we'll just have to agree to disagree." Our only ruling authority (and it can be a grim, authoritarian one at that) is the unholy trinity of "I, me, and myself." The test of our Sunday worship becomes the question "Can you feel it?" Whatever Wesley thought about his experience at Aldersgate, he probably didn't think about experience as we think (feel) today!

He meant that the Holy Spirit, having done a mighty work in the creation of the world, in the raising of Christ, now did a confirming, assuring, engaging work in warming his heart to the truth of Jesus Christ. Wesley's was an experience of something outside the bounds of his limited experience, even his well-formed experience—an Other coming to him, grasping his life, commandeering toward places he could not have gone on his own. Thus Wesleyans would praise the gift of a warm-hearted "assurance of salvation" as a most gracious gift of a constantly reaching Holy Spirit who does not let us doubt or be confused about where we stand with God. This God, through the Holy Spirit, comes out and gets us, even at church meetings.

"Life in the Spirit" involves diligent use of the means of grace such as praying, fasting, attending upon the sacraments, and inward searching in solitude. It also encompasses the communal life of the church in worship, mission, evangelism, service, and social witness.

That phrase *diligent use of the means of grace* makes some of our fellow Christians nervous. Aren't we saved by God's gracious gift of salvation, not by our diligent doing? Might we be in danger, in using God's gifts, of abusing those gifts? All that can be true, yet here we come upon a distinctive United Methodist emphasis. God's grace, to be gratefully received by us, is also given to be responded to by us. Experience of the Holy Spirit not only warms our hearts; it also strengthens our hands and puts our feet in motion. We are saved by Christ in order to walk with Christ. Christ serves us in dying for us on the cross so that we might serve him in our living and dying for him. Grace, for United Methodists, is not a warm, coddling embrace of the permissive God who says, "I love you just the way you are. Promise me you won't change a thing." Grace for us is always God's gift of power to live transformed lives in service to God. We may come to God singing, "Just as I am, without one plea," but this active God never stops creating all things new, including us. We never walk away from encounters with this God the same as how we came.

Fortunately, God means for us to be changed, converted, and renewed, but the Trinity doesn't mean for us to do or be anything "on our own." God gives us, in Wesley's wonderful words, "means of grace" that strengthen us and prod us along the way. The *Discipline* gives a helpful list—***praying, fasting, attending upon the sacraments, and inward searching in solitude***—though we are free to add others or to neglect some of these, in accordance with the needs of our souls. In calling spiritual disciplines like praying, fasting, receiving the sacraments, and inward, solitary searching "means of grace," we are saying that these acts are not simply something that we do but something that God does with us. For instance, most of us are conditioned to think of prayer as something that we do—as what we say to God. But what if prayer is meant to be considerably more conversational? What if prayer is mostly what God says to us? When we pray, we are attempting to put ourselves in that location where God can get to us, which may be one reason why we don't pray more often!

And the sacraments? We sometimes talk about "doing" the Lord's Supper or "performing" a baptism. But United Methodists join most of the universal church in thinking of sacraments as "means of grace" whereby God does for us and performs gracious work in us. In these activities, God is busy acting upon us, placing something in our empty hands, enlivening our cold hearts, enabling us to be transformed in ways that we could never be on our own. As a United Methodist pastor, one of the most moving moments for me comes when my people come forward to receive the bread and the wine of communion (a typical Methodist practice) and I see them hold out their hands for the bread. It takes the church to teach us that unnatural gesture. What's natural are hands clutched and grabbing, holding on tight, closed. The church teaches us to open up, to admit our hungers, and to expect God to give us what we need. How typical of Jesus to celebrate the whole meaning of his ministry, in a communal meal—a sign of communion and community, need and nourishment, hospitality and love.

We begin our journey with Jesus in baptism. Baptism catches up, in water and the word, all that you must do and say, all that

God says to you and does in you, in order to follow Christ. The name "Father, Son, and Holy Spirit" is laid upon you. Note that baptism is something that is done to you rather than by you. Baptism is an odd, radical sign that you can't fully follow Jesus without, in the Holy Spirit, being washed, done over, drowned, saved, and enlightened—dying to yourself and rising to a new you (the images are all biblical ones for baptism). Yet there is also your response. In baptism, we inquire into what you believe, asking you to state your faith before God and the church, using the words of the baptismal confession of faith, the so-called Apostles' Creed. We also testify to what we the church believe, telling you that we are hereby adopting you, initiating you into Christ's church, saying that we look at you and see an incipient disciple of Christ.

That's one reason why United Methodists, like the majority of Christians down through the ages, continue to baptize the babies of Christian parents. A baby—helpless, unknowing, utterly dependent and vulnerable—is a nice reminder that that's the way all of us look when we stand before God. No matter what our age or our expertise in discipleship, we're going to need grace to make it. "While we still were sinners, Christ died for us," Paul says (Rom. 5:8). He could have as easily said, "When we were helpless, unknowing, vulnerable infants, Christ died for us."

We are initiated and incorporated into this community of faith by Baptism, receiving the promise of the Spirit that re-creates and transforms us.

Through the regular celebration of Holy Communion we participate in the presence of Jesus Christ and are thereby nourished for faithful discipleship.

We therefore believe that our churches ought to celebrate Holy Communion often and robustly. John Wesley stressed the necessity for "constant Communion." We never get so adept at living the Christian life, so full of faith, so finished in repentance, that we are not hungry for God's word and in need of God's grace as the Holy Spirit continues to work in us. And every baptism becomes a renewal of your own baptism, a reminder that you are in this faith because the Holy Spirit worked in someone to put you there, to tell you the story, to live the faith before you until you could, in the power of the Holy Spirit, take it up for yourself. Salvation is a corporate, communal phenomenon. In saying, "I believe," you are not making some heroic, individual statement. You join your voice with others. Baptism is a sign that the Holy Spirit has a more considerably expanded notion of "family" than that which is dominant in our culture. No one expects you to believe, to witness, to serve, or to have faith alone.

And don't worry about trying to remember all of this! Just keep attending church and receiving the sacraments, listening to Scripture read and Scripture preached, singing the songs we will teach you, and enjoying the means of grace that the saints have enjoyed before us, and we promise that you will, in the power of the Holy Spirit, make it home. Thus Jesus said of the holy mystery of the Lord's Supper, "Do this in remembrance of me." Just do it. These are the means of grace that preserve us from doctrinal amnesia.

Life in the Spirit . . . also encompasses the communal life of the church in worship, mission, evangelism, service, and social witness. Earlier in this chapter, we noted that United Methodists believe that the Holy Spirit helped form the church for purposes that are beyond the bounds of the church. We said that *the church, which the Spirit has brought into existence,* is used by God *for the healing of the nations.* We thus have a very functional view of the church and its purpose that was inscribed in us by the Holy Spirit. Why did American Methodists found nearly three hundred schools, colleges, and universities, some of the finest in this nation? Why, in out-of-the-way places all over America, are there more United Methodist churches than U.S. post offices? Why are some of the most-vital and largest predominantly African American denominations also named "Methodist"? Why are there millions of Methodists throughout the world, on every continent, growing by leaps and bounds, especially in Africa and Asia? How did we get one of the largest church publishing houses in the world, and why did we build a large office building to lobby and to educate politicians on Capitol Hill in Washington, DC? What were Methodists doing marching in demonstrations and having rallies for women's right to vote, for child labor laws, for civil rights legislation, and nuclear disarmament?

Answer: United Methodist pneumatology.

4

We Believe in Christ's Universal Church

*M*any people today adore Jesus, admire his teaching, are inspired by his example; they just can't stand Jesus' friends, the church. They esteem the spirit of Christ, but they are turned off by the body of Christ. I understand their discomfort. After all, I spend most of my life in the church, so I know a thing or two about the church's pitiful shortcomings. Spiritually sensitive people can believe that Jesus Christ may be the Savior of the world, but they are disturbed by the way that Jesus got physical in the church.

Alas for us American rugged individualists, the church, for all its sorry infidelities, is the form that the risen Christ has chosen to take in the world. If we are to believe in Christ, we've got to believe in him as he is—embodied and embedded in the church—rather than in some disembodied form that would make Christ easier for us to handle.

One of the curious things about the risen Christ was not simply that Jesus, who was once dead, was now alive. The oddity was where he went and what he did immediately after his resurrection. Read about it in John 20. The risen Christ did not appear before any of the wise and the powerful, the political and the authoritative, which would have been a good strategy for winning the world. What better strategy than to reveal himself to those who had some power to make something happen in the world?

No, he was not only raised from the dead, but he returned to his disciples. That is, he came to the very ones who had so disappointed and betrayed him, that ragtag group of buffoons who had so poorly understood and much less followed him in his earthly ministry. Jesus rose to the church. Paul says that Jesus uses the stupid and the trashy to subvert the world's wisdom:

> Consider your own call, brothers and sisters: not many of you were wise by human standards, not many were powerful, not many were of noble birth. But God chose what is foolish in the world to shame the wise; God chose what is weak in the world to shame the strong; God chose what is low and despised in the world, things that are not, to reduce to nothing things that are. . . . He is the source of your life in Christ Jesus. (1 Cor. 1:26–28, 30)

Paul is talking about us, the church. These half-understanding, fearful, disappointing disciples—Jesus breathed on them, empowered them with his Holy Spirit, and sent them out to do the work that he himself did (John 20:26–29). It's a heck of a way to begin a revolution. So United Methodists say in our *Discipline:*

We understand ourselves to be part of Christ's universal church when by adoration, proclamation, and service we become conformed to Christ.

Note that all these statements from the *Discipline* are in the plural: "*We* understand"; "*We* believe." It is more typically American to speak in the first-person singular. We are a nation of individuals. Well, church is God's appointed means of helping us to get over all that. Church is where we go to learn to look up and to reach out beyond the confines of our subjectivity, to lay down our preoccupation with ourselves and join a family, a movement—to be adopted by the body. Church is where we learn to call strangers "brother," "sister." Note that Jesus didn't just call a conglomeration of isolated individuals. He called a group of twelve disciples. Get it? He was re-forming the scattered twelve tribes of Israel, gathering God's dispersed family. Jesus thereby indicated that the narrow way he was calling people to walk was too demanding and difficult, too delightful and adventuresome, to walk by ourselves. The Christian faith is a group thing.

"All Praise to Our Redeeming Lord," which praises the gift of "social grace," was one of Charles's hymns for the celebration of the Love Feast. The Love Feast was a service borrowed from the Moravians as a sign of the unity and love in the church:

Let us join ('tis God commands),
Let us join our hearts and hands;
Help to gain our calling's hope,
Build we each the other up.
God his blessing will dispense,
God will crown his ordinance,
Meet in his appointed ways,
Nourish us with social grace.
(1780 *Hymns*, #507)

Connected

We now turn to a cardinal United Methodist way of being Christ's church—*connectionalism.* United Methodists are, in our organization and church life, connected. At first glance, our connectionalism may seem like an organizational or managerial technique rather than a theological affirmation. True, if you say "connectionalism" to the average United Methodist, that person will probably think first of the bumblings of bishops, the machinery of clergy appointments, committees, rules, bureaucracy, and other ecclesial mechanisms. Sometimes it has been difficult to tell the difference between Methodism and the machine. Our two American founders, Bishops Francis Asbury and Thomas Coke, in explaining the purpose of the *Discipline* to American converts in 1798, even bragged that these rules would help birth a church "in order and in motion" like "the wheels of the vast machine."[1] One nineteenth-century Methodist swelled with pride as he boasted that the American West was conquered by two great mechanical inventions: James Watt's steam engine and John Wesley's church!

At our best, a connectional church meant that we could do things together—all churches bound by mutual responsibility and support—that we could never have done alone. At our best, connectionalism meant that we cared for our ties with the church catholic and joined hands with other Christians where possible. At our best, our connection has been a marvelously resourceful means of deploying clergy where they were most needed to help accomplish the mission of the local congregations bound together in

United Methodism. Methodism began as a covenanted association of lay preachers, committed to one another to work together to "spread scriptural holiness throughout the land." Indeed, our church today frequently refers to itself simply as "The Connection."

At its worst, connectionalism meant a church plagued by slow-moving ecclesial bureaucracy and stewardship reduced to a simple matter of paying "apportionments" (the general church's assessment of each local congregation for its "fair share" of the costs of running the mission, benevolent, and administrative work of the church at large). Clergy membership in "The Connection" has been reduced to "appointments" that are doled out by a sort of tenured preacher union and "apportionments" cheapened to a franchise fee that is charged to local congregations for the privilege of using the cross-and-flame logo on their buildings. Sad.

At our best, connectionalism has meant that our church puts great stock in regular gatherings (conferences—general, jurisdictional, annual, district, and church) where we gather to sing, pray, testify, and move forward the work of the church. Through these regular meetings, our church stays connected, renders account to one another, deploys for mission, and keeps encouraging itself to more effective discipleship. John Wesley even listed "Christian Conferencing" as a "means of grace," which is a lot to claim for a church meeting, but at our best, our meetings have been not only meetings with one another but meetings with our Maker, that is, a "means of grace." When the mundane work of a church meeting ascends to the thrilling worship of the living God, that's grace.

I could list all of the ways that I think our Connection needs to be more adaptive, flexible, efficient, and productive in its meetings and conferences; more supple in its clergy appointments, apportionments, and other means of connectionalism; but I won't bore you with such organizational details. Why go negative? Besides, we have, in our recent history, tried to renew our connection by tinkering with the ecclesiastical machinery, which has usually resulted only in more complicated and even less productive machinery. One of the sinful lures of connectionalism is to delude us United Methodists into thinking that our problem is better machinery when it is the prejudice of this book that anything that would generate real renewal in the church is at heart theological.

Now is a good time to note that connectionalism is the organizational embodiment of some wonderfully invigorating key theological convictions. By being part of the Connection, we demonstrate our belief that there is no such thing as an "independent" congregation—from the beginning of the Christian faith, churches were tied to one another as closely as they were yoked to Christ. Read the letters of Paul, and you find this early leader of the church not only strengthening local congregations in their ministry but also strengthening their connection to and responsibility for one another. That's a major reason that we have bishops—to insure the catholicity and connectivity of the church. We have superintendency of our clergy and our churches to insure that we are responsible and accountable to one another in Christ. We have appointed, that is, *sent* clergy to keep making clear that the function of clergy is in leadership of the mission of the congregation and that they must keep that congregation tied to the larger mission of the universal church. Our clergy are therefore accountable not only to the local congregation but to The Connection. Our connection is a way of affirming our catholicity and our responsibility under the mandates of Christ.

Also, as we noted at the beginning of this book, our United Methodist ideas of God are thoroughly Trinitarian; therefore our church organization must be thoroughly relational. A key aspect of the Trinity—Father, Son, and Holy Spirit—is relationship. Just as Father, Son, and Holy Spirit are one, so are we bound, as branches to a vine (John 15:2–4), to the love of God in Christ, and so does the love of God bind us to one another. As Jesus says, no branch bears fruit by itself (John 15:4). This God loves to connect. Something within this faith is deeply communal and relational, that is, connectional.

Members of the Universal Church

We understand ourselves to be part of Christ's universal church.
. . . You may have noted, in our belief statements in the *Discipline,*

a studied effort on the part of United Methodists to be unoriginal, saying, "With other Christians we . . ." and "As part of the universal church. . . ." I'm almost embarrassed in this book to speak of "distinctive United Methodist beliefs." It's not because United Methodists are so bland that we blend in with the dominant doctrinal wallpaper, though sometimes we are boringly unexciting. It is rather that we are determined to be catholic in our believing. As we noted, John Wesley never desired to establish a new church. We are somewhat embarrassed that we ended up as a separate, distinct denomination. True, we are Protestant Christians, but we are Protestants with a bifocal commitment to the "holy catholic church" (as we say in the creed), that is, to the universal church. We want to believe what the whole church—the historic, orthodox, apostolic, catholic church—has believed at all times and places.

So in our worship we are both pietistic, free-church Protestants *and* sacramental, liturgical catholics. In our biblical interpretation, we both honor the Bible as the supreme, first, and final rule of faith (like most Protestants), *and* we honor the two-thousand-year experience of the church and its teaching (like most Roman Catholics). We have pastors leading individual congregations, *and* we have bishops leading individual pastors. Again, we see "conjunctive theology" at work in that little word *and*.

So we invite all Christians to join us when we celebrate Holy Communion; this is not a United Methodist table—it's the Lord's table, and he invites all. Our official services of worship are freely borrowed from the work of Catholics, Lutherans, and Anglicans. Our hymnody is derivative of other traditions, and many other churches sing more faithfully because they have borrowed from us the hymns of Charles Wesley. We have built into our church structure an ongoing imperative to be in dialogue with other Christians, and we will joyfully pray with them and worship God with them when invited, not because we don't take our theological commitments and differences seriously but rather because we take very seriously our firm belief that we are called to be visible witnesses to the essential unity of Christ's holy catholic church. We recognize the ministerial orders of other churches as well as the validity of their baptisms. As the Trinity is diverse yet unified, so we believe the church is meant to be. We really believe that when Jesus prayed for his disciples that they "may all be one" (John 17:22), he was talking about us, all of us. We pray and work for that day when Jesus' prayer will be realized in us. We really do want to be *conformed to Christ* in "one Lord, one faith, one baptism" (Eph. 4:5).

This also means that we test our *adoration, proclamation, and service* by the measurement of the universal church—what the church has everywhere taught, believed, and practiced down through the ages. We are willing to innovate and contemporize our worship, but we also know that the test of any practice is more than "do the people like it or not?" The true test is catholic—is this congruent with what the church has done at all times and places? So on Sundays, in our churches, you are likely to pray an Anglican prayer, sing a Baptist praise chorus, hear the choir sing a Lutheran chorale, get theology from the pulpit that sounds somewhat Presbyterian, and celebrate it all with the Lord's Supper and a Prayer of Thanksgiving that is mostly indebted to the Catholics. Like John Wesley, we are eclectic, willing to learn from a wide array of fellow Christians and their traditions. As Lutherans love Lutheranism and its traditional music, as Presbyterians love the Reformed tradition's theology, so we United Methodists love to borrow from both the Lutheran and the Reformed. That's our tradition.

We have found it helpful not to prattle on too much about "our distinctive Wesleyan tradition" (writing a book on United Methodist beliefs has necessitated my laying aside our innate doctrinal modesty). We are inveterate borrowers, embracers, experimenters, and ancient-future spongers. We do this because we believe in getting help from our friends in our adoration, proclamation, and service. We do it all in order better to be *conformed to Christ.* Christ is too rich and wonderful, the Christian faith too complex, the assignments of discipleship too demanding, to do him justice without help from our friends. United Methodists are thus uniquely positioned when it comes to whatever form of the church may emerge in the future because of our ecumenical spirit.

The Kingdom of God

We pray and work for the coming of God's realm and reign to the world and rejoice in the promise of everlasting life that overcomes death and the forces of evil.

We United Methodists are "political" in that we really believe that when the New Testament calls Jesus "king," and when in all those places Jesus says, "The kingdom of God is like . . . ," he really means a place, a time when God finally gets what God wants from creation, when the intentions of God shall be fully realized. A kingdom implies boundaries, limits, some place that is under the reign of God as opposed to elsewhere that isn't. Thus we join other Christians in praying, in the prayer Jesus taught, "Thy kingdom come, thy will be done, on earth as it is in heaven."

And we can pray thus because we believe that, in Jesus Christ, in the church, some of God's kingdom has already come and some of God's will is already being done. "Church" is a word that denotes what a living God does corporately, communally, politically, and visibly in the world. We believe that the church, for all its blemishes, is a work of God, who loves us enough to push us toward community that we could not have on our own. Here is an account of the Pentecostal birth of the church:

> And suddenly from heaven there came a sound like the rush of a violent wind, and it filled the entire house where they were sitting. Divided tongues, as of fire, appeared among them, and a tongue rested on each of them. (Acts 2:2–3)

Our church isn't simply a helpful human institution for the betterment of humanity. Our church is "from heaven," the result of God's gracious intrusion into our affairs, a wind that blows apart our usual means of gathering people and thrusts us toward a new experience of giftedness and togetherness that is nothing sort of miraculous. Church is called to be a clear alternative to the way the world gathers people, a foretaste of the kingdom where social practices are pioneered that the world has yet even to dream.

Wesleyans have not been too worried about heaven and hell, the possibilities that await us in the hereafter, because we have tended (with the help of the church) to be more focused on God here and now. We really believe that "the kingdom of God has come near to you" (Luke 10:9). Jesus is enacting God's kingdom and God's will for the world right now, through ordinary (very ordinary) folk like us. The gift of Pentecost in the dramatic descent of the Holy Spirit in Acts 2 was a people who look different and who live differently:

All who believed were together and had all things in common; they would sell their possessions and goods and distribute the proceeds to all, as any had need. (Acts 2:44–45)

We also look back to the end time in which God's work will be fulfilled. This prospect gives us hope in our present actions as individuals and as the Church. This expectation saves us from resignation and motivates our continuing witness and service.

True, God's realm and reign are not here in its fullness, not by a long shot. Death and the forces of evil still have their way with too much of the world, and with too many of us. We are not there yet, but we have been given—through Scripture, through our experiences of God's coming kingdom in glimpses in the church—a vision of the last act of the drama. And that visionary experience *saves us from resignation and motivates our continuing witness and service.* That's one reason that John Wesley insisted not only that his followers be diligent in Bible study, attendance on the sacraments, and prayer but also that they were regularly in jails, working among the poor and the oppressed, the dispossessed and the downtrodden. There is a link between our views on heaven, our hope for the ultimate triumph of God, and our busyness in behalf of the kingdom of heaven here on earth.

Note that our sweeping assessments of faith in the goodness and power of God are tempered by honest admission that we are not right and the world is not right. As we have said, among the things that United Methodists believe is that we are sinners. Too many things happen in the world that can in no way be attributed to "God's will." It is important to be honest that the United States (with a military budget greater than all the military expenditures of all the other nations of the world combined), or any country for that matter, is not the realm and reign of God. Though Christ has died for us and redeemed us, our redemption is still in process. The church, as glorious as it sometimes is, is also at times an utterly human inglorious mess. When we work on our little lives and attack the world's big problems, we do so not in the misapprehension that we've got some minor tinkering to do to make basically nice people just a bit better; we are joining with Christ in going head-to-head with the principalities and powers. Organized sin and death are all around us, and we go so far as to call their names when we start listing the evidence of social and personal sin in our Social Principles in the *Discipline*.

We Wesleyans get our propensity to work on the kingdom from Wesley. Here's a sample from Wesley's *Journal* that gives you a sense that when Wesley says that we are given the gifts of the Holy Spirit, those gifts are meant to make us busy:

> We are enabled by the Spirit to mortify the deeds of the body, of our evil nature; and as we are more and more dead to sin, we are more and more alive to God. We go on from grace to grace, while we are careful to abstain from all appearance of evil, and are zealous of good works as we have opportunity, doing good to all men, while we walk in all His ordinances, blameless, therein worshipping Him in spirit and in truth, while we take up our cross, and deny ourselves every pleasure that does not lead us to God.[2]

Wesley's robust sense of grace as that work of God that works in us so that we might work for God puts Wesley at odds with much that passes for "spirituality" today, where we are urged to sit quietly and meditate on vague pleasantries. Wesley would probably dismiss much contemporary spirituality as mere mysticism, "quietism," sitting quietly in the expectation that God has nothing interesting for us to do with ourselves or in the world—which is one of the worst things Wesley could say about anybody. John Wesley didn't simply believe in grace; he believed in *responsible* grace, as Randy Maddox puts it, grace that empowers us to live new lives for Christ rather than for ourselves. Wesley stressed "participation" in the love of Christ, not merely reception.

With other Christians we recognize that the reign of God is both a present and future reality. The church is called to be that

place where the first signs of the reign of God are identified and acknowledged in the world. Wherever persons are being made new creatures in Christ, wherever the insights and resources of the gospel are brought to bear on the life of the world, God's reign is already effective in its healing and renewing power.

The work that we do as Christians and as a church is a witness, a sign, a signal that God's kingdom is coming. That promised realm is here at least incipiently in certain holy hints and momentary glimpses. The church exists in part to point us toward the outbreak of the realm and reign of God here and there and to help us find our places in that vast army of peace and righteousness. The other day a preacher and I were complaining to one another about the sorry state of the church and our aggravation with it. Then, after a long, dreary complaint from me, the pastor said, "You want to see the kingdom of Heaven?"

He took me down into his church basement where two older women were washing, drying, and neatly folding the clothes of the homeless people who lived on the streets around the church. These are the same women who, after they wash the clothes of the homeless, prepare them a nice meal for lunch. It was a United Methodist moment. You wonder if Jesus Christ is Lord? Well, try explaining the actions of those two women on any other basis than as an outbreak of the realm and reign of God.

Salvation

So what we believe about our life with God in any world to come is based to a great extent on our experiences of God—in worship, Scripture, church, and world—here and now. When the *Discipline* says that we *rejoice in the promise of everlasting life that overcomes death and the forces of evil,* we are pointing into the future, but we say this right after making a statement about the political significance of the gospel here and now.

Thus John Wesley was roundly criticized for talking about "full salvation," the completion of God's work in us as a present, mundane reality rather than a future hope and heavenly expectation. He didn't only hold justification and sanctification together—God's work for us and God's work in us—he also held together a future hope of God's triumph, with stress on present experience of that triumph here and now—which explains the *Discipline's* characterizing Christian hope as *a present and future reality.*

Wesley inherited from his Anglican background a theology of moral rectitude—our relationship to God is based in great part on our righteous actions before God. The church, so taught the Anglicans, was the mediator of grace for salvation through sacraments like baptism. Anglicans did a good job of asserting human responsibility for our relationship with God. In Wesley's case they did too good a job, for he took upon himself, in his young life, far too fastidious a form of piety. At Aldersgate, based on his own frustrating experiences to embody this rectitude in his own life, as well as the invasion of the Holy Spirit in his life, Wesley became a great advocate for the Lutheran idea that we are saved solely by the grace of God, not by our good works.

But will all be saved? Against both Calvinists and Lutherans, Wesley maintained a firm confidence that our ultimate destination is a matter of God's work in us *and* (there's that little conjunction again) our response to that work. Against Pelegian optimism ("We're all basically nice folks who are making progress") and Augustinian pessimism ("We're totally depraved sinners who can make no contribution to our redemption"), Wesley steered a typically Anglican middle way, but with a bit more traction than the Anglicans had been able to make out of the matter.

Whereas Calvinists stressed "predestination"—God elects (that is, chooses) and predetermines some for salvation, some for damnation—in his own life Wesley had discovered God to be richly resourceful and determined. The way Wesley figured it, if Jesus Christ could die for a priggish, know-it-all little sinner like him, there's little limit to whom Jesus would die for.

Yet Wesley's expansive theological imagination also combined his rather Lutheran stress on justification through faith in God's work in Christ with an Arminian theology that lauded God's gracious work in us and despite us. (James Arminius was a sixteenth-century Dutch pastor and scholar who outraged both Calvinists and Lutherans with his stress on the need for human response to

God's work.)[3] Wesley, as an Anglican heir of Arminius, saw human sin as more of a malignant disease than as total, complete depravity. ("Salvation" means, in the original, "healing.") The universal cure for so serious a malignancy was God's universally offered grace powerfully working in everyone. Wesley therefore stressed prevenient grace more than he talked about election, a stress that he probably received from his own Anglican heritage, mixed with a dash of pietism. Prevenient grace leads us (we'll say more about this later), sometimes gradually, sometimes dramatically, in fits and starts and through slow progression, toward genuine repentance and renunciation of our efforts to save ourselves ("I can't save myself; you'll have to do it in me") and toward real faith ("I know that Jesus Christ has saved and is saving me"). All this is gift, said Wesley, and it is universally offered.

What Wesley heard read at that church meeting at Aldersgate Street in 1738 was Martin Luther's *Preface to the Epistle to the Romans*. But a couple of years later, when Wesley got around to a careful reading of Luther's *Commentary on Galatians*, he didn't like at all what he took to be Luther's irrationalism and antinomianism (anti-law). In his dislike of Luther's too-rigid distinction between gospel and law, he was closer to Calvin than Luther. Still, he liked the Calvinists' predestinationism even less, which he saw as their excuse to lapse into antinomianism. For Wesley, law *is* gospel when it is the law of the love of Christ, working in us through the Holy Spirit, to the glory of the Father.

What's new here is Wesley's great confidence in God's grace to accomplish its intentions. But God's grace is not irresistible. Grace gets God's foot in the door with us; grace enables us to be honest about our sinful situation; grace enables us to say "yes" to God in faith; *and* grace enables us to live sanctified, holy lives. Wesley used 1 Corinthians 1:30 over seventy times in sermons during the first six months of his English Revival: "He is the source of your life in Christ Jesus, who became for us wisdom from God, and righteousness and sanctification and redemption, in order that, as it is written, 'Let the one who boasts, boast in the Lord.'" It is Wesley's stress on "to live sanctified, holy lives" that kept his theology from ever being "universalism." He raised the bar on salvation rather than sentimentally lowering it, seeing our salvation as begun and completed by the work of Jesus on the cross, a work done for all, yet he also saw it as a long process that takes one's whole life to bring to full fruition.

For someone close to Wesley to say, "I have been saved" is to say, "I have been enlightened, set free *and* . . . given a demanding, lifetime assignment by God." As Wesley put it (borrowing from Saint Paul), "sin remains but no longer reigns."[4] That's one reason that United Methodists named our successful program of Bible study "Disciple." We didn't name it "Thinking Long Thoughts about Scripture" or "Discovering Key Bible Truths to Help You with Your Life." We called it "Disciple." We study the Bible as a means of grace whereby we are better enabled to enact the Bible in our discipleship. As noted earlier, for the heirs of Wesley "discipline" is not a dirty word.

The Calvinists were concerned that Wesley had described the way of the elect as too perilous and conditional. Wesley responded that because the way of faith was always a risky journey, spiritual disciplines and practices are absolutely essential. God does not expect sinners like us, even as redeemed sinners, to walk this way without help. Therefore God graciously gives us certain "means of grace" like *adoration, proclamation, and service,* whereby, wonder of wonders, even people like us, still tied to the realms of evil and death, *become conformed to Christ.* Now you understand why Wesley was into "practical" as opposed to speculative or theoretical theology. We have been justified (saved, made right with God) in order that we become sanctified (made holy, righteous by God).

Although I said at the beginning of this chapter that we United Methodists do not have a great desire to be distinctive, this Wesleyan linkage of faith and good works, of justification by faith and sanctification through faith and works, can be said to be a distinctive Wesleyan contribution to the church catholic. Justification is what God in Christ does for us; sanctification is what the Holy Spirit does in us. Wesley believed that through the Holy Spirit a deep change in character is worked in the faithful believer. He loved 2 Corinthians 5:17: "If anyone is in Christ, there is a new creation." John Wesley took that promise of new creation with absolute seriousness, seeing his own life and the lives of thousands of ordinary Methodists as validation of the apostle's sweeping statement of faith.

As his brother Charles taught Methodists to sing:

Finish, then, thy new creation; pure and spotless
Let us be. Let us see thy great salvation
Perfectly restored in thee; changed from glory
Into glory, till in heaven we take our place, till we
Cast our crowns before thee, lost in wonder, love, and praise.
(United Methodist Hymnal, #384)

To be honest, Methodist ecclesiology, our doctrine of the church, is a bit schizophrenic. On the one hand, we struggle with the legacy that the Wesleys set out to reform an established church, not to establish a new church. We were a lay renewal movement within the Church of England. On the other hand, out of Wesley's frustrations, disappointments, and rejections by his fellow Anglicans, Methodism became a new church, first in America, then throughout the world. Although he and Charles died as priests in the Church of England, John Wesley also died frustrated by the unwillingness or inability of his beloved church to respond to the legitimate evangelical challenges that were being posed by the "people called Methodists."

While remaining a committed Anglican and sacramentalist churchman, Wesley introduced a number of innovative, extraecclesial practices to help to feed the spiritual hungers of his Methodists in the societies. His essentially practical and pragmatic nature took over as Wesley eventually stooped to some fancy theological footwork in securing the services of an orthodox bishop to ordain some of his preachers. Eventually, he ordained some preachers himself for work in Scotland and America, claiming that if the Anglicans wouldn't respond to the need, he would himself. He was thereby on his way to founding a new church, attributing his unorthodox moves, as one would expect of Wesley, to the movements of God's grace.

Today, as the church in North America finds itself amid new challenges and difficulties, and as being a Christian in this culture begins to feel more like being a missionary in hostile territory, ecclesiology takes on new significance. On the one hand, United Methodists have a healthy respect for the need for stable, carefully thought-out organizational embodiment of the love of Christ in order for the church to do the work of Christ. On the other hand, we've got reformism and radical renewal in our bones and when our institution becomes ossified, we get edgy and contentious, knowing that God has called us for more than the form without the spirit. Our Wesleyan missional impulse makes us feel guilty when we hunker down behind our church doors; yet our Wesleyan love for the historic, catholic witness of the faith renders us discontent with merely mirroring whatever the culture happens to be responding to at the moment.

Perhaps this is a gift we have to offer the church catholic: our ecclesial schizophrenia.

5

We Believe in Practicing Theology

*I*n 1780 John Wesley sent to his American Methodists (his "poor sheep in the wilderness") a hymnbook, full of brother Charles's hymns, a *Collection of Hymns for the Use of the People Called Methodist.* In the preface he praised the hymnal as "a little body of experimental and practical divinity," claiming that these were not just uplifting songs but also practiced theology, beliefs in action through music. About the highest compliment that Wesley paid a belief, a theology, a hymn, or an individual Christian was this— *practical.*

Wesley wasn't much of a speculative or theoretical thinker; the ultimate test of an idea was its practical force, its incarnational applicability. To that end he spent much care crafting liturgies, devising sermons, and composing hymns. Did you note at the beginning of this book that Wesley's sermons, as well as his rules for the conduct of his societies, were some of our major resources for theological authority? Theology sung, said, and lived by believers was the theological contribution of Wesley, the pastoral theologian par excellence. If you couldn't live an idea as a hymn of praise to Christ, why think it? To this day, any big theological assertion isn't of much interest to us United Methodists if it can't be sung, body and soul.[1]

When asked, "How do we know that Jesus is the way, the truth, and the life?" Wesleyans tend not to trot out our big theological arguments but rather our disciplined little lives. While we know that Christ's truth is not dependent on our ability to embody it, we also know that the best assertion of Christian truth is in the sort of

/ 59

lives it produces. In this incarnational faith, the point is embodiment; it is performance as much as intellectual assent. Theological affirmations are meant to be practiced.

Theology is our effort to reflect upon God's gracious action in our lives. In response to Jesus Christ, we desire to be drawn into a deeper relationship with the "author and perfector of our faith."

Theology is more than our collective ideas about God, some creative human conceptual thrusting out into the void. Rather, theology is reflection on what God is doing among us, on the ways in which God has self-revealed to us in the past and here and now. All faithful God talk is therefore responsive and reflexive, something done by God to us before it's anything thought by us. Theology is what God says about God.

Don't miss the countercultural impact. We live in a culture that judges all events and experiences on the basis of what they do for us. So there is a tendency to come to church asking, "What do I need to do?"; "How will this be helpful in my life?"; "What am I feeling now?" We say we are there for the theology when, in truth, it's mostly anthropology, humanly derived thoughts about human dilemmas.

So in defining theology as our reflection on *God's gracious action in our lives,* we United Methodists are saying that theology is not so much our talk *about* God but God's talk *to* us; it is God's self-revelation, not simply our self-derived projection. We do this through *study, reflection, and prayer*—not through long walks in the woods or by delving more deeply into our psyches but rather by receptive, patient listening of the sort that you are doing now as you read this book, listening for a word that you could not have come up with on your own. Prayer. First Jesus Christ is busy among us, then we reflect on his work with us, desiring *to be drawn into a deeper relationship* with the One who has so graciously drawn toward us.

Practicing Faith

We think theologically in order that we might live theologically, putting into practice our claims about the world now that the Word has become flesh and moved in with us. Therefore, *our theological task includes the testing, renewal, elaboration, and application of our doctrinal perspective in carrying out our calling "to spread scriptural holiness over these lands."* Wesley offered a thumbnail definition of Methodist purpose: "to spread scriptural holiness over these lands." We think theologically in order to have something faithful to say about Jesus and in order to have a faithful way of living for Jesus that is clear, convincing, and effective. Other church families would be more concerned that their theology was orthodox, or historically valid. Typical of us pragmatic Wesleyans, we want ours to be "effective."[2]

Jonathan Edwards (a Calvinist!) put it this way:

> Passing affections easily produce words; and words are cheap; . . . Christian practice is a costly laborious thing. The self-denial that is required of Christians, and the narrowness of the way that leads to life, don't consist in words, but in practice. Hypocrites may much more easily be brought to talk like saints, than to act like saints.[3]

To be honest, sometimes our United Methodist pragmatic, practical Christianity slips into mere cultural accommodation: American pragmatism that values what the world thinks now more than what the church has historically taught. In disputes over doctrine or ethics, rather than ask, "Is this faithful to our United Methodist way of thinking?" we settle for "How will this play in Peoria?"

There once was a time when Methodists had strict stands against divorce, the use and abuse of alcohol, and other issues that we considered to be violations of our call to be a holy people. Did we adjust our thought on these matters because we received new and different revelation or because we decided that our thought was more than the market could bear? In my humble opinion, the current United Methodist statements on issues like abortion, war and peace, and homosexuality—to mention a few of our more muddled statements—are more representative of the ethos of our culture than our distinctive ways of Wesleyan believing. Pragmatism, that peculiarly American philosophy, for any of its virtues, tends to begin and end with the status quo, the world as it is and we as we are. Not much transformation and conversionist thinking in that. When "practical" becomes "pragmatic" the faith once delivered to the saints too easily degenerates into "this is about as much of Christian believing as we can take at the moment."

In his 1768 *Christian Library,* Wesley's compendium of Christian thought for all Methodists, Wesley's controlling criterion for his selection was "Is the thought of this person truly practical?" Is it helpful in the formation of Christians? But when he selects some church father to quote, Wesley clearly prejudices the thought of the martyrs like Polycarp, Clement, and Ignatius—they paid for their thought with their blood. Belief in the truth tends to provoke the world when it is put into practice by ordinary people. When Wesley said "practical," he didn't mean "Christianity made painless."

So let's be clear: in extolling "practical divinity," Wesley meant not "what works for us" but rather those doctrines that wondrously, sometimes painfully, always miraculously transform our modest little lives into the sanctified lights to the world that God intends us to be.

I don't know whether the next statement in the *Discipline* is meant as a slam against academic, speculative theologians of the sort who burrow in a college department of religion, but the *Discipline* says, ***Our theological task is essentially practical. It informs the individual's daily decisions and serves the Church's life and work. While highly theoretical constructions of Christian thought make important contributions to theological understanding, we finally measure the truth of such statements in relation to their practical significance. Our interest is to incorporate the promises and demands of the gospel into our daily lives.***

So strong a defense of practicality has sometimes made Methodists seem anti-intellectual. How can a church that was born on the Oxford University campus, a people whose father is no less an intellectual than John Wesley, a church so committed to higher education, be called antiintellectual? Sometimes we haven't been faithful to our scholarly roots, to be sure. But sometimes the problem is in the world's limited definition of "intellectual" or "theological." We United Methodists like to think that we are committed to a wider, more responsible rationality that sees our theological ideas as practical commitments whose truth is tied to their embodiment.

Wesley took the idea of small accountability groups from the European pietists and developed them into the engine that drove the Methodist revival in England. He was no revivalist, blowing through town, blowing off, and then blowing out. He said that he was resolved "not to strike the hammer down in any one place where I could not follow up on the blow." He formed "societies," large groups of smaller groups ("classes," from ten to twenty people); and "bands," small intimate groups (four to six people) where there was intense accountability and encouragement for these ordinary, everyday eighteenth-century English people to become nothing less than saints. Some believe that Wesley's greatest theological contribution was not his written theology but rather his institutionalized, organizational embodiment of his ideas in these "classes," where people lived the theology that Wesley proclaimed.

From our Anglican roots United Methodists got the notion that *the living core of the Christian faith was revealed in Scripture, illumined by tradition, vivified in personal experience, and confirmed by reason.* Scripture, tradition, experience, and reason— these are four means of theological reflection (sometimes referred to as the "Wesleyan quadrilateral" because John Wesley employed the four in his thinking[4]) and the criticism of our practice of theology. Note that Scripture is the first of the four, *revealing the Word of God "so far as it is necessary for our salvation."* By "tradition" we Methodists mean that which was thought and taught by the church at all times and places before we got here—that rich, bubbling inheritance from the teachers of the church; the creeds, hymns, and prayers that guide us and preserve us from having to reinvent the wheel, spiritually speaking, in each generation. Reason is our active, thoughtful, analytical engagement with this biblical and traditional material, that confirmation of revealed truth within our own thought about the world, since this is, in truth, God's world. Experience[5] is that personal and communal confirmation of the reality and the work of the triune God in our lives, the way in which God's creative, transforming, revealing work is demonstrated and made undeniably real in our own lives.

Tradition reminds us that we are not the first to walk with Jesus as disciples, and we walk not alone. The saints guide us. Christianity did not leap from the New Testament into our hands; twenty centuries of witness guide us in our contemporary appropriation of this faith. We meet no great idea in this faith that our forebears did not think before us, and, conversely, we struggle with no heretical bad idea in the contemporary church that did not bedevil the church before we got here. We had tradition before we had Scripture, for Scripture is the faithful expression of the experience of those who were Israel and the first church. Yet with other Protestant Christians we regard Scripture as a judge of the fidelity of the church's tradition and a constant source of cross-examination of tradition.

We therefore find that one of the weaknesses of some forms of contemporary spirituality is that they are, well, *contemporary.* They are little more than with the times, merely a current expression of present ideas. Superficiality is the inevitable result of a failure to think with the saints.

Early Methodist preachers were accused of fostering dangerous innovation. They responded that they preached the historic faith of the Church of England as found in the Articles of Religion (which are still printed toward the beginning of our *Discipline*), the Anglican Homilies (a collection of authoritative sermons from great Church of England preachers), and the *Book of Common Prayer.* Wesley's followers saw themselves not as creative innovators but as faithful traditionalists who were recalling the Church of England to its historic affirmations.

Not long ago a woman told me that she had a long struggle becoming close to Jesus. She had meditated, prayed, and read. Then she happened upon a history of the Methodist movement in Britain and from that she concluded, "When a Methodist is apart from the poor, a Methodist is just not much of a Methodist." That insight, derived from an encounter with tradition, led her to commit to a prison ministry that goes into women's prisons and prays with and for the inmates. "Those women have made a true disciple of Jesus out of me," she said. So don't tell us United Methodists that history is about the dead ideas of dead people!

One blessing of thinking as a United Methodist is that our theology is constantly challenged and enriched by a confluence of various historical traditions—most recently, the marriage of the Evangelical United Brethren Church and the Methodist Church (1964). And we have the blessing of being a worldwide, global movement. Our earlier world-mission efforts are bearing fruit in our present interaction with young, vital Methodist-related churches around the world. So when we gather for General Conference to talk doctrine and program, we gather as believers with a wide array of cultures and histories that speak a dozen different languages. The enrichment of our theological reflection by the witness of those who have suffered oppression and who have not shared the Western, North American church experience enriches and enlightens the received tradition of the church in the West.

Experience is our recognition that God's grace impacts and guides individual lives and is also a means of theological reflection. We say that the Bible is "God's word," but that word is never spoken in a vacuum. We each hear God's speaking in the context of our own culture and social location. Fortunately, the Trinity is polyphonic and multilingual.

In John 9:1–25 a man is cured of blindness. Immediately there is a theological dispute concerning Jesus' ability to heal and to teach. "Who sinned, this man or his parents, that he was so afflicted?" Jesus' critics ask.

Jesus doesn't really answer their interrogation; rather, he points to the glory of God in this man's healing. As for the man who was healed, he testifies, "All I know is that once I was blind, but now I see" (John 9:25). The man speaks from his experience of Jesus' powerful grace. Experience is a testimonial to our faith in the living, resurrected Christ and the power of the Holy Spirit at work in us. Of course we have doubts and misgivings about various aspects of Christian testimony; who doesn't? But amid our doubts, we have at our best always been able to say, "All I know is, that once I was blind, but now I see." Our God is a God of the living and not the dead (Mark 12:27), and experience is our validating, confirming, and enlivening encounter with a living Lord.

By Reason we read and think through Scripture; we try to gain clarity and precision about the mystery of God with us; we test our declarations of faith by the witness of tradition; and thereby we affirm that all truth is of God. Thus United Methodists have never thought that education and learning were threats to faith, considering it our Christian duty to support hundreds of colleges and universities. True, we know that we are sinners and sometimes our sin infects and distorts our thinking, so our reason isn't to be used alone and unaided (nothing a Christian does is to be done alone and unaided), but reason is often a help in critically testing and discerning the fidelity of our thought. A sovereign, creative, truthful God is not threatened by our human attempts to describe and better to understand the nature and purposes of God. Of course, our various practices of "reason" are culturally, historically, and personally conditioned and limited. Whatever we think "reasonable" must be tested by the tradition of the church and above all by Scripture, which is the tradition, reason, and experience of those who have come before us. Reason is a divinely given gift that enables us to appropriate God's gracious revelation.

The Primacy of Scripture

Yet it would be a real distortion of United Methodist theology to claim that this quadrilateral is equilateral. In the *Discipline* the first source of theology is Scripture. Scripture is clearly—in Wesleyanism and in us—primary:

We share with many Christian communions a recognition of the authority of Scripture in matters of faith, the confession that our justification as sinners is by grace through faith, and the sober realization that the church is in need of continual reformation and renewal.

Many have noted a "crisis in authority" in contemporary life. Once revered sources of authority—family, elders, science, government—are now under suspicion. Scripture has a privileged place in our thought. The first place that we turn whenever we have some doctrinal dispute or argument about ethics is to the Bible— the received, revealed wisdom that is Scripture. And the last word in any of our debates over faithfulness is Scripture.

More than that, we believe that Scripture means to have practical authority over our lives as Christians. Think of Christian thinking, in great part, as lifetime training in how to submit in thought and in action to the authority of Scripture. I say "lifetime training" because that's usually how long it takes to take the Bible a little more seriously and ourselves a little less so. Most of us come to the Christian faith already in the grip of other authorities—our peers, our social class, our gender, our nation, our race—the list of our masters is long.

The ability to say, "The Bible shows us that . . ." is therefore not as ingrained in us as the tendency first to say, "My best friends believe that . . ." or "As a loyal American I believe . . . " or "Science has proven. . . ." We dismiss the authority of Scripture as too limiting, too archaic, and too constrained by cultural context—which proves what a great challenge it is to free ourselves from the authorities that are in charge of our lives in our present cultural context. What we call "freedom of thought" is often a testimonial to how happily enslaved we are in present intellectual constrictions. The restrained, limited "modern worldview" has got us. So we open up the Bible and say things like "It's so violent!" (an ironic thing to say about the Bible for someone who is a member of one of the world's most violent cultures). Or we point with condescension toward the sexism or racism that we suspect in the Bible. (It is so much easier to see the Bible's cultural limitations than our own.) We have not thereby freed ourselves from the Bible's limitations so much as we have demonstrated our own cultural blinders.

So one of the most-radical, truly countercultural acts that we perform in Sunday worship is that of gathering and then opening an ancient book—written in languages quite unlike our own, by people from cultures very different from ours—and we become silent, and we listen to the word read and proclaimed and thereby we say to ourselves, "These ancient Jews knew more than we."

John Wesley had a vivid sense of Scripture as a talking book. In his first collection of published sermons, *Sermons on Several Occasions,* Wesley said that he aspired to be "a man of just one book." With Wesley we believe that through this collection of ancient writings, God has uniquely spoken to the people of God. John Wesley taught that Scripture is "God breathed." God—Father, Son, and Holy Spirit—speaks to us today through Scripture.

Though a few confused United Methodists may have been "literalists" or "fundamentalists" in their reading of Scripture, we have never officially been so limited. We have too much respect for our dependence on the Holy Spirit in our scriptural interpretation, a healthy acknowledgment of the distance between Scripture's originating context and our own situations, and a too-vivid sense of the reality of a living, resurrected, and revealing Lord. We have found that the Bible's word is enlivened through scholarly study rather than muted and that the word the Bible speaks is always multivocal, thick, lively, relevant, and rich:

We are aided by scholarly inquiry and personal insight, under the guidance of the Holy Spirit. As we work with each text, we take into account what we have been able to learn about the original context and intention of that text. In this understanding we draw upon the careful historical, literary, and textual studies of recent years, which have enriched our understanding of the Bible.

Note that I'm discussing the Bible in the context of "practical theology." That may sound strange. One of the chief complaints about the exhortations and the guidance of Scripture is that the Bible is just not relevant (that is, *practical*) to our needs and concerns today. We hear the words of Scripture and think, "Well, that all sounds great, on paper, but in the real world, it won't work." So much for the authority of Scripture. When we hear Jesus in the Scriptures (which is the primary way we hear Jesus) saying to "turn the other cheek" or to "forgive seventy times seven," we are conditioned to reply, "Get real!" In other words, one of our most-persistent and conventional ways of resisting the authority of Scripture is to say, "Get real, Bible."

But that begs the question of who defines reality. The Bible intends to be more for us than just a book of rules, a repository of helpful principles for better living. Attempts to use the Bible like that are bound to be frustrated by the nature of the Bible's way with the truth. Scripture is an attempt to construct a new world; to stoke, fund, and fuel our imaginations. The Bible is an ongoing debate about what is real and who is in charge and where we're all headed. So the person who emerged from church one Sunday (after one of my most-biblical sermons, too!) muttering, "That's the trouble with you preachers. You just never speak to anything that relates to my world" makes a good point.

To which the Bible replies, "How on earth did you get the idea that I want to speak to your world? I want to rock, remake, deconstruct, and rework your world!"

When it comes down to it, there are few rules and regulations in Scripture and very few principles for better living. Most of the Bible is stories, narratives of the way that God has been with the saints. The practical authority of all this is to renarrate our world in such a way that we emerge from church on a Sunday—after hearing the word read, preached, and interpreted—rubbing our eyes and scratching our heads because we have been moved to a very different world and a distinctively different way of naming reality—God's world, God's way.

Our standards affirm the Bible as the source of all that is "necessary" and "sufficient" unto salvation (Articles of Religion) and "is to be received through the Holy Spirit as the true rule and guide for faith and practice" (Confession of Faith).

So when someone says that Scripture, contrary to the way United Methodists see it, is impractical and unrealistic, tell them that what they probably mean is that Scripture is difficult and demanding. When we read Scripture, allow it to have its authoritative way with us, and submit to its peculiar way of naming the world, we are being changed, transformed, sanctified in the hearing. God is breathing an enlivening Holy Spirit upon us; Jesus is speaking directly to us; and a new world is being created by the Word. It's Genesis 1 all over again.

Thus when we read Scripture, we're not simply to ask, "Does this make sense to me?" or "How can I use this to make my life less miserable?" but rather we are to ask in Wesleyan fashion, "How would I have to be changed in order to make this Scripture work?" Every text is a potential invitation to conversion, transformation, and growth in grace. And, as we have noted earlier, we

Wesleyans love to get born again, and again. Perfected. Scripture is God's appointed and most frequently used means for getting to us and getting at us and thereby changing us in the encounter.[6]

It may therefore be helpful in thinking about Scripture not to envision yourself picking up this ancient, hard-to-understand, and impenetrable conglomeration of documents but rather to see a living God coming out to get you, remaking you, giving you new eyes with which to see yourself and the world.

If you have ever been sitting there in church dozing contentedly through the reading of Scripture and the following sermon, only to be suddenly seized, commandeered, grabbed by some insight not your own, some word spoken to you from the outside, some flash of brilliance, well, you have just had what we call *a recognition of the authority of Scripture in matters of faith.*

Thus our affirmation of the primacy and the authority of Scripture is quickly followed by a statement on the ministry of all Christians: *We affirm the general ministry of all baptized Christians who share responsibility for building up the church and reaching out in mission and service to the world.* We think in order more effectively and faithfully to be in ministry. Theology is too important to be left to the professional theologians, and ministry is too essential to be left to ordained pastors. In fact, by baptism we are all "professional theologians," every one of us, because we profess Christ. We want to be that which we profess. We want to do that which we think. We want to be those on whom Jesus will one day look with joy and say, "Well done, my good and practical servant."

The General Rules remind us that salvation evidences itself in good works.

Earlier I mentioned that one source of our United Methodist beliefs is the General Rules, which were written by Wesley after he expelled sixty-four persons from the Newcastle society in February of 1743. Joining a Methodist society required that persons have "a desire to flee from the wrath to come, and to be saved from their sins."[7] How is that to be done? Wesley devised the General Rules for that purpose.

The General Rules arise from the Wesleyan conviction that

Christian doctrine ought to form Christian character. The General Rules are thus not simply practical but also transformative—a helpful, daily way that ordinary people can work out their own salvation with fear and trembling (Phil. 2:12). The rules prohibited everything from buying or selling slaves, to drunkenness and dealing in alcohol, "quarreling, brawling, brother going to law with brother," "unprofitable conversation," and "laying up treasure upon earth." One by one, the heirs of Wesley have let many of these rules fall by the wayside. Yet even today they remind us that discipleship is a matter of practical embodiment of the implications of the love of God in Christ.

The General Rules represent one traditional expression of the intrinsic relationship between Christian life and thought as understood within the Wesleyan tradition. Theology is the servant of piety, which in turn is the ground of social conscience and the impetus for social action and global interaction, always in the empowering context of the reign of God.

As we say in the Watch Night Service covenant that is still used among United Methodists:

> Christ has many services to be done; some are easy, others are difficult; some bring honor, others bring reproach; some are suitable to our natural inclinations, and temporal interests, others are contrary to both. In some we may please Christ and please ourselves; in others we cannot please Christ except by denying ourselves. Yet the power to do all these things is assuredly given us in Christ, who strengthens us. . . . Let us now, in sincere dependence on his grace and trusting in his promises, yield ourselves anew to him.

"Practical Christianity" is a means of yielding ourselves to Christ.

6

We Believe in Transforming and Perfecting Grace

*W*hen the *Discipline* gets around to using the word *distinctive* to describe us not-too-peculiar United Methodists, it uses *distinctive* most frequently and persistently to describe our views about something called "grace." It is not an overstatement. If you must know something distinctive about United Methodist believing, then look to our emphasis on the grace of God in Jesus Christ and the way that grace works in our lives.

Grace pervades our understanding of Christian faith and life. By grace we mean the undeserved, unmerited, and loving action of God in human existence through the ever-present Holy Spirit.

The Greek word in the New Testament that is translated as "grace" (*charis*) means simply "gift." Our relationship to Christ is instituted by his gift of himself, and it is sustained through countless gifts of love that generate, through the Holy Spirit, gracious holy living. We exist with God—Father, Son, and Holy Spirit— every moment of our lives, every step of our life's way, only by gift.

Pick up the morning newspaper and read of wars, rumors of war, and so many acts of cruelty and destruction. The world can appear to be a cold, chaotic, and indifferent place. Yet United Methodists believe quite optimistically that beneath all that and despite all that **God's grace is manifest in all creation.** Moving restlessly behind the scenes, sometimes seen and experienced, often ignored and overlooked, is the Creator who made us and the world and who is determined to get it all back. The same Creator who loves to make something out of nothing has graciously called people like us to be

72 /

in *covenant partnership with God. God has endowed us with dignity and freedom and has summoned us to responsibility for our lives and the life of the world.* If God partners with the likes of us, then God must be extremely gracious, giving, and forgiving. Fortunately for us, we have a God who loves to make something out of us nothings. We name this godly creativity "grace."

Paul, writing to the bitterly divided, love-deficient First Church Corinth and after hammering them for more than a dozen chapters for their shortcomings as a church, finally asserts to them the matter of "first importance":

> For I handed on to you as of first importance what I in turn had received: that Christ died for our sins . . . that he was raised on the third day . . . that he appeared to Cephas, then to the twelve. Then he appeared to more than five hundred brothers and sisters at one time. . . . Then he appeared to James, then to all the apostles. Last of all, . . . he appeared also to me. (1 Cor. 15:3–8)

Here is the foundation of the church, the rationale for faith, the matter of greatest import: *the risen Christ appears to us.* That first Easter, nobody actually saw Jesus rise from the dead. They saw him afterwards. In the Bible, the "proof" of the resurrection is not the absence of Jesus' body from the tomb; it's the presence of Jesus to his followers. The message of the resurrection is not first "Though we die, we shall one day return to life." It is "Though we were as good as dead, Jesus returned to us." If it was difficult to believe that Jesus was raised from the dead, it must have been almost impossible to believe that he was raised and the very first thing he did was to come back to sinful, dead-from-the-neck-up people like us.

The result of Easter is the church—a community of people with nothing more to convene us than that the risen Christ returned to us and gave us his mission. That there is a United Methodist Church today is in itself a sort of validation of Easter faith. Something there is about this Trinitarian God that is relentlessly self-revealing. Show us what God looks like! we demanded of Jesus (John 14:8). God? God is the shepherd who doesn't sit back and wait for the lost sheep to head home. God goes out, risks everything, beats the bushes night and day, and finds that single, lost sheep.

We thought that with the blood and the betrayal of Friday, it was the end. We thought it was over between us and God. At last, we had gone too far, had stooped to the torture to death of God's own Son. It's over.

Then on Easter, he came back, and we realized that the cross wasn't the end of the story between us and God but rather its beginning. Christ came back to *us*.

Christians are the people who don't simply know something the world does not yet know, or believe something that non-Christians don't yet believe. Our faith is not first a matter of what we believe; it's a matter of something that God has done. God has shown up and continues to do so, even when we're not expecting or looking for God. We are the people who have had something happen to us that the world appears not yet to have experienced. We live not alone. As Paul says, it is what is most important. God—Father, Son, and Holy Spirit—keeps showing up.

Prevenient, Justifying, and Sanctifying Grace

While the grace of God is undivided, it precedes salvation as "prevenient grace," continues in "justifying grace," and is brought to fruition in "sanctifying grace."

[Prevenient grace] is the divine love that surrounds all humanity and precedes any and all of our conscious impulses. This grace prompts our first wish to please God, our first glimmer of understanding concerning God's will, and our "first slight transient conviction" of having sinned against God.

Prevenient (literally, "coming before") grace is the gift of God's work in us before we know that God is working in us. Prevenient grace is that strange but wonderful way that God intrudes into each life, convincing us of our need, awakening us to God's presence and gracious availability to us, strangely empowering us to be better for God than we could have been had we been on our own. Prevenient grace is an affirmation that if we see, and if we believe, and if we follow, it is gift, all the way down. For instance, if you read in the opening chapters of this book my somewhat turgid discussion of the mysterious doctrine of the Trinity, and if you say, "I get it! I believe!" you do so not on your own intelligence or volition. We believe that it's gift, grace, revelation, and testimony to God's work within you. Even to be able to say that faith is not an achievement but a divine gift is itself a divine gift.

In yet another example of Wesley's Trinitarian thought, he defines *prevenient grace*:

> If we take this [salvation] in its utmost extent it will include all that is wrought in the soul by what is frequently termed "natural conscience," but more properly, "preventing grace"; all the "drawings" of "the Father," the desires after God, which, if we yield to them, increase more and more; all that "light" wherewith the Son of God "enlighteneth everyone that cometh into the world," showing every man "to do justly, to love mercy, and to walk humbly with his God;" all the convictions which his Spirit from time to time works in every child of man.[1]

There are few more countercultural assertions for those of us who are "mother-I'd-rather-do-it-myself," self-help North Americans than a belief in prevenient grace. We tend to think of religion as something that we do for God or something that we believe about God rather than primarily, preveniently what God believes about us and has done in us, despite us. We think that we have come to church because we wanted to be there and that we are following Jesus because we heroically summoned up the courage to follow. We strut about pompously thinking that the lives we're living are our own.

What if your life is not merely the sum of your choices, wise and foolish, but also God's loving choices for you? Prevenient grace is typical of the atoning ("at-one-ment") of Jesus Christ. There is something about a Trinitarian God that constantly wants to make a way to us, despite us. God takes the antecedent step toward us and enables any responsiveness from us. Charles Wesley gave wings to the prevenience of grace when he wrote,

> Long my imprisoned spirit lay,
> Fast bound in sin and nature's night.

> Thine eye diffused a quickening ray;
> I woke, the dungeon flamed with light.
> My chains fell off, my heart was free,
> I rose, went forth, and followed thee.[2]

In Alcoholics Anonymous the decisive first step toward recovery is the admission that an individual cannot, on one's own, work one's recovery. There must be recognition of bondage to alcohol. Yet even that recognition is a gift, often the unwanted gift of the intervention of others who love the alcoholic. We must be enlightened to our true situation from the outside, by another. That's grace. After recognition there comes the huge step that moves us from awareness to an exercise of the will and actually doing something about our enslavement. And, as AA demonstrates, that too is a step that can only be made with help from the outside, not only with help from the group of fellow alcoholics but also from the "higher power" that enables us to do that which, on our own, we could not do. This is close to what Wesley meant by prevenient grace.

There is grace in admitting that God's prevenient grace is a major explanation for who you are and where you are headed. Too often we present the Christian faith as a problem to be solved: believe this, do that, feel this, think that. It's hard work being a follower of Jesus.

But prevenient grace says that God Almighty is busy working in your life, sometimes subtly, often dramatically; pulling, pushing, convicting, and encouraging; tugging; doing something decisive about the problem of you. As Jesus said, "You didn't choose me, I chose you that you should go and bear fruit in my name" (John 15:16).

Early Methodists never tired of giving testimonials to the transforming power of God's prevenient grace in their lives. "I was lost, then I got found" is the theme that runs throughout these testimonies. They were bold enough to claim their own lives as irrefutable, concrete evidence of God's love reassuring them, making them new people. The gospel intends to discipline us, that is, to save us, to transform us, to do a good deal more within us than simply to civilize us. When the apostle Paul looked back over his own encounter with Christ on the Damascus Road, he knew not whether to call what happened to him "death" or "birth": it felt like both at the same time.

It's difficult to say at some moment in your life, "God is leading me to do this at this time and place," though that may certainly happen. More typically for us, in the backward view, is to say, "Wow. I thought I went to that Bible study last night out of habit, only to discover that the Holy Spirit was bringing me to a place I would have never gone by myself!" That's grace, and it is not only amazing, as we sometimes sing, but also prevenient.

Grace is the engine of our salvation. Wesley's great concern was "salvation," or the more theological "soteriology." Wesley had a bit-more-complex notion of just what it means for us to "be saved" than some of his theological predecessors (and many of his successors!). The classic Wesleyan text on soteriology is his 1765 sermon "The Scripture Way of Salvation." He opened this sermon with a definition:

> What is *salvation*? The salvation which is here spoken of is not what is frequently understood by that word, the going to heaven, eternal happiness. . . . It is not a blessing which lies on the other side of death . . . it is a present thing . . . [it] might be extended to the entire work of God, from the first dawning of grace in the soul till it is consummated in glory.[3]

Salvation is much more than momentary assent to some biblical truth, and much more than a legal transaction that guarantees the recipient eventual heavenly bliss. Christ's work on the cross is not only pardon from sin but also power to live new lives now. Salvation in Wesley is a journey, a largely therapeutic process that Albert Outler characterized as a movement from the *barely* human, to the *truly* human, to the *fully* human.[4] While this movement could possibly be instantaneous in a soul, more than likely it is gradual growth in response to God's grace, in which we daily learn to die and to rise with Christ. From his own observations of the working of transforming and perfecting grace in the lives of early Methodists, Wesley came to appreciate the diverse ways in which the Holy Spirit transforms a life. Toward the end of his life, Wesley advised Mary Cooke,

> There is an irreconcilable variability in the operations of the Holy Spirit on [human] souls, more especially as to the manner of justification. Many find Him rushing in upon them like a torrent, while they experience "The o'erwhelming power of saving grace." . . . But in others He works in a very different way: "He deigns His influence to infuse; Sweet, refreshing, as the silent dews." It has pleased Him to work the latter way in you from the beginning . . . in a gentle and almost insensible manner. Let Him take His own way: He is wiser than you; He will do all things well.[5]

One of Wesley's great achievements in soteriology was to keep a vital tension between God's grace and our grace-driven but never-forced involvement. The Wesleyan theologian Randy Maddox calls this "responsible grace." By this formulation, says Maddox, Wesley maintains primary focus on God and God's actions without obliterating human responsibility.[6]

A word of theological caution: When we Wesleyans speak of this triumph of prevenient grace, there is the danger that such talk will overshadow our truthful and orthodox assertion of the pervasiveness of human sin. How do we affirm with the Western theological tradition (thanks to Augustine against the Pelagians) that we are indeed sinners utterly unable to save ourselves from our sin? How do we avoid hedging on the historic affirmation that salvation from sin belongs only to God in Christ, working through the Holy Spirit without our help or encouragement, and (with Wesley) assert that God has given us the freedom to take some real responsibility for our situation?

We do it through our belief in prevenient grace.

Our sin, while obvious and undeniable, is not the last word on the human condition. God didn't stop creating after the first six days of creation. God continues to get involved in each life, giving grace that enables all of us, despite our sin, to say—when confronted by the presence and work of Christ—"yes."

To be honest, sometimes we United Methodists don't always succeed in maintaining honesty about our sin and God's grace, our freedom and God's work, or God's initiative and our response. Sometimes we back off from our sober view of human nature, acting as if our sin were not, after all, so serious. We lapse into Rousseau-inspired romantic notions that we are, after all, naturally good people who, having no need for moral transformation, await the flowering of our innate goodness. Or we reduce God's grace to a helpful nudge, a spark that awakens the best in us, a technique to follow in order to get better—"bootstraps theology" or "prosperity theology" in its peculiarly American form. Or we say that salvation occurs only in the best and the brightest, the fortunate few on whom the grace of God has especially shined—that is, Gnosticism—the spiritually elite, the truly good plucked from the rabble of the rest of you who can go to hell. Many non-Christians justifiably find such self-righteousness to be repugnant.

In his sermon "The Witness of Our Own Spirit," Wesley says that grace is "the power of God the Holy Spirit working in us." Grace is not a substance to be measured out to us but rather a relationship that God in Christ establishes and maintains with us in the Holy Spirit. Behind anything we United Methodists say about the grace of God is a stout view of God. When compared with the contemporary, rather tamed and constrained deistic God who slumbers on the sidelines of the modern world, Wesley has a robust sense of God's agency. Wesley's God is constantly at work, making a way where there was none, intruding, creating, enticing, miraculously moving us closer to our Maker and Savior.

Justifying Grace

Justification and assurance are the ways we speak about the accepting, pardoning love that meets us in Jesus and his cross and resurrection and the way that we name the decisive change that comes when we are given an awareness of that justification through the work of Jesus Christ.

Scripture—Old Testament and New—is a story of undeserved, unmerited, unexpected grace, of new beginnings and a fresh start that is given by God. When Christians say "justification" we mean that we have been assured, through the Holy Spirit's vivification of the truth of this story in our lives, that in Jesus Christ, God was doing something decisive about our sad situation. We, who were nobodies, became somebodies; we who had no future with God because of our sin and rebellion were given a future. We who had wandered into a far country (Luke 15) were sought, found, saved, and brought back from the dead.

In justification we are, through faith, forgiven our sin and restored to God's favor. This righting of relationships by God through Christ calls forth our faith and trust as we experience regeneration, by which we are made new creatures in Christ.

The experience of this justifying grace is "conversion." We delight (in Wesley's way of putting this) in "new birth." We enjoy decisive breaks with the hackneyed old and a resolute entrance into the creative and the novel. Deep in our Methodist souls is the memory of that priggish little Oxford don who got empowered at Aldersgate Street. After that Aldersgate experience, Wesley logged 225,000 miles, mostly on horseback, and preached some 40,000 sermons, converting an estimated 140,000 in his lifetime and many more after his life ended. He wasn't just warmed; he was ignited.

Yet we Wesleyans tend not to think of conversion (as some American evangelicals have thought) as an instantaneous, one-time event. For us, transforming grace tends to be experienced as a long process of transformation, of gradual growth in grace and sanctification. We believe that "moving on to perfection" tends to be lifelong and that we rarely get so mature in the faith, so perfected and holy, that God has no more growing for us to do.

And when we are converted, made over, it is because of what God does, not what we do. One of Wesley's most evocative images was the thief on the cross (Luke 23:43). Wesley portrays this man who is promised, "Today you shall be with me in paradise" as the paradigmatic instance of justification.[7] The man did nothing, believed in almost nothing, yet when he turned to Jesus, Jesus turned completely toward him, promising him a place in his kingdom. That is pure justification, said Wesley, a pure work of God, and it is grace.

Such a change may be sudden and dramatic, or gradual and cumulative. It marks a new beginning, yet it is part of an ongoing process.

Wesley stressed an "assurance of salvation"—the Spirit "bears witness with our spirit that we are children of God." I wonder if modern people are as troubled about their salvation as people in Wesley's day. Wesley's stress not only on justifying grace but on "assurance" of that grace reminds us that our salvation is not totally dependent on how we think, feel, or act. Salvation, justification to God, being made right with God, is gracious gift of God. The church exists joyfully to proclaim that in Christ, God was and is reconciling the world to himself (2 Cor. 5:19). We are able to love God boldly because in Christ, God has first boldly loved us. We need not spend our lives with God anxiety-ridden, full of consternation and caution, worried about just where we stand with God. We don't need constantly to be taking our spiritual temperatures, relentlessly scanning every step that we take, troubled that we may have messed up. We know whose we are. Wesley loved to cite Romans 8:15–16: "When we cry 'Abba! Father!' it is that very Spirit bearing witness with our spirit that we are children of God." We are thus assured of God's resourceful, adopting love for us. Wesley puts it this way:

> The testimony of the Spirit is an inward impression on the soul, whereby the Spirit of God directly "witnesses to my spirit that I am a child of God"; that Jesus Christ hath loved me, and given himself for me; that all my sins are blotted out, and I, even I, am reconciled to God.[8]

And how do we know that our assurance is not merely our self-assurance? Wesley stressed the marks of salvation, the visible "fruits of the Spirit." If there is spiritual fruit, evidence, results, then there is spiritual assurance. For Wesley this was a widely attested, obvious scriptural truth: disciples ought to look, act, and sound like their Master. A Christian is someone who, at least to some visible degree, actually walks and talks like Jesus.

Sanctifying Grace

Justification is not the end of the story. There must also be "fruits of repentance," response to the work that God has done in us in our justification. As Wesley describes the relationship of justifying and sanctifying grace, "our main doctrines, which include all the rest, are three: that of **repentance,** of **faith,** and of **holiness.** The first of these we account, as it were, the **porch** of religion; the next, the **door;** the third is **religion itself.**"[9]

In affirming sanctification as strongly as justification, Wesley parted company with aspects of traditional Lutheran and Calvinistic teaching on justification[10] and, depending on how you see it, placed himself at odds with traditional Protestant theology of salvation or made a brilliant contribution to the continuing exploration of divine truth! He appreciated Calvin more than Luther on the issue of sanctification. Of Luther he said,

> Who has wrote more ably than Martin Luther on justification by faith alone? And who was more ignorant of the doctrine of sanctification or more confused in his conceptions of it?[11]

Wesley, whose own heart-warming assurance at Aldersgate demonstrated the gifted quality of justification by faith alone, was never able to preach just faith alone. To faith he added—as confirmation of and stimulus to faith—spiritual disciplines, practices, and good works. Claims of justification without evidence of sanctification were what Wesley called "dead religion." If one neglected good works toward God and neighbor, Wesley thought that it was possible, indeed probable to "backslide," to forfeit the good work of God in you by neglecting good works for God. Use it or lose it was Wesley's view of grace.[12]

To those who charged Wesley with that dreaded Protestant anathema "salvation by works," he countered that any good work we do, before or after justification, is due to the grace of God working in us through the Holy Spirit. Faith without good works is not really faith, for faith is always known by its ability to produce, even among foul sinners like us, truly good fruit. He thus refused to contrast faith with good works. The two go together, or faith is not faith, and our works are not really good. By the sanctifying grace of God we are sanctified, made holy, so that for the first time in our lives we are free to actually do something good for God and neighbor. By the gracious disciplining of our lives to God, our lives are healed and made more true to God's originating intentions for us. To our surprise and delight, we wake up to find ourselves miraculously moving in the same direction as God, working with the grain of the universe because God is working in and through us. We are startled to find that we want what God wants, and our desire is gradually consumed by a desire for God's will to be done on earth as it is in heaven.

Wesley found a way to avoid the Reformation tendency to contrast "faith alone" with "holy living." "Conjunctive theology" is what we earlier named as this Wesleyan tendency to join two theological assertions that were otherwise kept rather separate and distinct. He combined classical Augustinian affirmations (a strong sense of original sin, a vivid appreciation for the sovereignty of God) with a joyful Christian ethic of human responsiveness that sometimes sounds almost Eastern Orthodox in its blissful celebration of the restoration of the once-defaced image of God in us. In his evangelistic message Wesley joined justification and regeneration with sanctification, avoiding both vaunted human self-assertion and human ethical passivity. As Albert Outler characterized Wesley, "he turned out 'rules' by the dozen—but also with warnings that even the most scrupulous rule-keeping will get you only to the state of being an 'almost Christian.' He developed intensive small group nurture and therapy for Christian maturation . . . all of these were elements in his larger project: to describe and promote the Christian life as rooted in faith *and* fruiting in love."[13]

Perfected in Love

Wesley taught genuine Christian perfection in this life, taking with straight seriousness Jesus' "Be perfect, therefore, as your heavenly Father is perfect" (Matt. 5:48). For Wesley, this astounding assertion toward the end of Jesus' Sermon on the Mount was not so much an impossible command as a gracious promise:

> How wise and gracious is this, to sum up, and as it were seal, all His commandments with a promise, even the proper promise of the gospel, that He will put those laws in our minds and write

them in our hearts! He well knew how ready our unbelief would be to cry out, This is impossible! And therefore stakes upon it all power, truth, and faithfulness of Him to whom all things are possible.[14]

This sort of Wesleyan sanctificationist talk drives many Lutherans, Calvinists, and Baptists through the roof. It seems to them naively deluded at best; spiritually self-righteous and arrogant at worst. To be honest, we heirs of Wesley have not always been able to keep these two truths—justification and sanctification—juggled in the air at the same time. Yet when we do, we are not only true to Wesley's theological legacy; we are also making a wonderfully visible Christian witness to the power of God's grace not only to save sinners but also to enable them to act like they are saved.

Sanctification and perfection are the most controversial and contested of United Methodist beliefs. From the earliest days of our movement, most Christians and their churches agreed with us on most matters of belief, but here we parted company. With the exception of the Greek Orthodox and the Roman Catholics and their teaching on sainthood, we Wesleyans were almost alone in our teaching about full sanctification—though the saints are few among the Orthodox and the Catholics. John Wesley believed that God's grace was so amazing and fruitful that it was possible, even for wretched sinners like us to get better, to "grow in grace," even to be "perfected in love." Ordinary people could be saints.

A reminder: Wesleyan sanctification is never our own moral achievement; it is an amazing work of God's grace in us. Gift, pure gift. Wesley defines "salvation" as actual, present transformation:

By salvation I mean, not barely (according to the vulgar notion) deliverance from hell, or going to heaven, but a present deliverance from sin, a restoration of the soul to its primitive health, its original purity; a recovery of the divine nature; the renewal of our souls after the image of God in righteousness and true holiness, in justice, mercy, and truth.[15]

The Christian life is never static, fixed, and final; it is always a progression toward God and neighbor. What matters, said Wesley, is that we are "going on to perfection." "Holy living" is God's love perfected in us as we testify to that divine work through our love of God and neighbor. Wesley understood "perfected" not in the sense of a sinless state of moral completion but rather in the sense of being mature, with sure signs of a visible progression in our fulfillment of God's intentions for our lives.

In 1785 Wesley published a sermon titled "On Working Out Our Own Salvation," in which he picks up on a phrase in Paul's letter to the Philippians: "Work out your own salvation with fear and trembling." He uses it as a defiant (against just about everything that had been taught in the orthodox Protestant—Lutheran and Calvinist—traditions) linkage of justificationist "faith alone" and sanctificationist "holy living." In a 1790 sermon Wesley talks about "The Wedding Garment" (from Jesus' parable of the Great Banquet in Matt. 22:2 ff.). A great feast is given and invitations are issued. Shockingly, the first invited refuse their invitations and make all sorts of bogus excuses for not accepting the invitations from the Lord of the Banquet. So the rebuffed host sends out his messengers, who go out and bring in the maimed, the blind, the lame, the outcast, and the oppressed. This is a narrative of God's amazing grace, says Wesley.

The story continues. One of the guests gets into the worst sort of trouble because he shows up without a "wedding garment." Inappropriately dressed for the feast, he is cast out. In good Anglican, sanctificationist fashion, Wesley interprets the parable as a statement that although we are invited to God's feast "just as we are," on the basis of nothing but God's gracious invitation, there is also a demand for "holy living," growth in grace. He asks, "What is the 'wedding garment' in the parable? It is the 'holiness without which no man shall see the Lord.' "

With other Christians we agree that we are saved—justified, made right with God—through the work of God in Christ on the cross and resurrection of Jesus. But with Wesley we have also given stress (though not equal stress, because our work is never equal to God's work) to the saving need for human response—repentance and the "fruits of repentance." We come forward singing, "Just as I am, without one plea," but God never leaves us as we are. That's sanctification.

In my experience, sanctifying grace is a promise for which many people today 'are hungering. They don't simply want to believe; they long for personal transformation through their believing. They don't want just to gather and praise God; they long for renovation, a "total makeover," as the popular TV shows proclaim. Having attempted self-enhancement, self-realization, self-actualization, and self-improvement and having been frustrated by their failed efforts at self-renovation, they want some means of living more abundant lives that are not purely self-sustained. Only a God who miraculously works in us can satisfy our transformative desires.

Contemporary mainline Protestants like the United Methodists are mistaken when we are embarrassed by the miraculous in Scripture and in the tradition of the church. Miracles—surprising works of God among us—are at the heart of the Christian faith.[16] Your life in all its twists and turns toward God is a miracle—that is, a mysterious but undeniable work of a creative God.[17]

I recently overheard two people talking: "Well, I'm Catholic; you're Methodist. That's fine. Whatever works for you," said one of them.

The other replied, "You must not know much about Methodists. It's not working *for* me; it's working *on* me. I'm really not a loving, peaceable person by natural inclination. If I'm going to act in a loving way toward the people I despise, God will have to make me that way."

Methodist sanctificationist, I love you!

That Wesley chose to describe this miraculous, God-initiated gracious work as "perfection" raises questions. Wesley never denied that even in our assured justification and most advanced sanctification, we make mistakes and have sinful inclinations, moral cowardice, and spiritual torpor. Yet even in our continuing inclination to sin, Wesley taught that we can be "perfected," made spiritually mature and freed from outward sin. It is even possible to be free, to a marked and amazing degree, from sinful thought and inclination instantaneously. While God does not simply impute holiness within us—we must respond in a disciplined way to God's grace working in us—Wesley's thought on grace is intensely miraculous. The same Jesus who was miraculously raised from the dead is able to raise us as well to levels of moral and spiritual life that we could never have without God's constant intervention.

You can imagine the political, social effect of Wesley's stress on perfection, sanctification, and assurance of salvation. Historically, the doctrine of original sin had sometimes been abused to keep the economically, politically oppressed in their lowly situation of oppression. Certain social sins—alcoholism, family breakdown, violence, thievery—were alleged by some of the powerful rich to be most pervasive among the powerless poor. The relatively well off and the educated seemed to have fewer problems with some of these sins, so they must be more virtuous. Why struggle against unjust economic and political structures when the poor, even out of their poverty, are going to be just as thoroughly sinful after their economic liberation as before?

Wesley's contention that *all* (not just the poor) had sinned and fallen far short of the glory of God *and* that *all* (not just the educated and the privileged) could also be redeemed and sanctified by God had a way of uniting rich and poor in their sinful status before God and in the possibility and promise of their salvation. People, no matter their lack of education or the limitations of family background, no matter their poverty or addiction, could hope for genuine triumph in their battles with evil. Therefore, many poor and dispossessed were encouraged and empowered in the early Methodist societies. And a number of the rich were incensed by the implications of Wesley's perfectionism. One wealthy grande dame scornfully castigated those infamous

Methodist preachers [whose] doctrines are most repulsive and strongly tinctured with impertinence and disrespect toward their superiors, in perpetually endeavoring to level all ranks, and do away with all distinctions. It is monstrous to be told that you have a heart as sinful as the common wretches that crawl on the earth. This is highly offensive and insulting.[18]

From the first, John Wesley was criticized for many of the emphases that we have examined in this chapter. For one thing, Wesley makes original sin, the pervasiveness of evil, and the primacy of pride such a huge part of his theology that these become the main problem that Jesus came to "solve." Compare Wesley's sweeping assertions about human sin and Christ's atonement with the Apostles' Creed or the Nicene Creed. You will likely see that all this Wesleyan emphasis on sin and redemption from sin seems an overemphasis. The creeds stress the full sweep of the work of the Trinity rather than simply our misdeeds and what is done about our sin.

Still, when one compares Wesley on sin and redemption with many of our modern, "Progressive Christian" notions of the human situation and its cure, you must grant Wesley's unfailingly honest portrait of the human condition in our sin as well as his constantly robust conviction of the resourceful, gracious work of God for us (justification) and in us (sanctification). By keeping salvation an exclusive work of God and by maintaining the undeserved, gifted nature of God's grace, Methodists maintain the free sovereignty of God while naming that sovereignty primarily as an exercise of complete, active, resourceful, and transforming love.

The Wesleyan, sanctificationist roots of our theology, at their best, have a way of keeping United Methodist theology, well, *theological*. Our astounding anthropological (i.e., dealing with our humanity) claims about the miraculous ability of God to perfect us in grace arise out of our full-bodied, gutsy theological claims. No merely human, psychologically, or sociologically derived programs for human betterment and perfectability can lead to the miraculous assertions of the triumph of grace that we find in United Methodist doctrine. If God did not raise crucified and dead Jesus to life, and if that same resurrected Christ did not actually come back to his frail followers, then our doctrinal claims are silly.

God's work for us and in us in transforming and perfecting grace was what John Wesley called the "way of salvation." The way of salvation is the good news that God in Christ, in the power of the Holy Spirit, keeps doing good work in us as we respond to God. In Christ, God commandeers our lives, all of our lives, in a way whereby we are not only forgiven the huge debt that we have run up with God but also enlisted and equipped to join with God in God's redemptive work in the world. Our right relationship with God is not only restored by God's grace, but we become by God's grace agents for the kingdom. We are adopted into a peculiar gathering of the gracious and graced that is named "church"—a visible, structured foretaste of the full kingdom of God to come and a constant means of grace to us in our journey with the living Christ.

7

We Believe in Faith and Good Works

We see God's grace and human activity working together in the relationship of faith and good works. God's grace calls forth human response and discipline.

As Wesley encountered resistance to his revival, he issued an "Earnest Appeal" to his critics, attempting to explain Methodism:

> This is the religion we long to see established in the world, a religion of love and joy and peace, having its seat in the heart, in the inmost soul, but ever showing itself by its fruits, continually springing forth, not only in all innocence . . . but likewise in every kind of beneficence, in spreading virtue and happiness all around it.[1]

Note that Wesley refuses to commend his revival exclusively on the basis of an experience that it engenders in its adherents. Nor does he take pride in the birth of a new institution or in his movement's conformity to the orthodox faith. He urges measurement of Methodism "by its fruits," by the "beneficence" it produces in the spread of "virtue and happiness all around it." Faith in Jesus engenders good works for Jesus. United Methodists join Wesley in joyfully linking the mercy of God with the holiness of God, what we believe with what we do, and who we are with how we act; and we pray that our doing will be a public testimony to the fidelity of our believing and will "spread scriptural holiness throughout the land."

Wesley's orientation toward the practical is evident in his focus upon the "scripture way of salvation." He considered doctrinal matters primarily in terms of their significance for Christian discipleship.

90 /

In Wesley's "Address to the Clergy," in which he outlined his expectations for the performance of his traveling preachers, he stressed (of course) *grace*—they should show response to God's work in their lives, *gifts*—they must show both God-given talents and acquired skills for ministry, and *fruit*—visible, measurable evidence of God's blessing on their ministry.[2] In countless ways, Jesus did more than ask us to "think this" or "feel this"; he also asked us to "*do* this." Faith is meant to be fruitful.

Whenever Wesley cited the deleterious results of teaching the doctrine of predestination, his main fear was that predestination fostered dreaded "quietism" and hindered the transformative work of God in the individual soul.[3] Wesley sneered that if people really believed in predestination, then "the elect shall be saved, do what they will: The reprobate shall be damned, do what they can."[4] The Christian life, initiated and sustained by grace, is known by its holy fruits.

The *Discipline* reminds us that ***Methodism did not arise in response to a specific dispute, but rather to support people to experience the justifying and sanctifying grace of God and encourage people to grow in the knowledge and love of God through the personal and corporate disciplines of the Christian life.*** Note that knowing precedes doing; experience of God leads to the service of God; and ethics arise out of doctrine. On the other hand, our knowledge of God is enriched and deepened in our service of God; our attempts to put the faith into practice encourage us to intellectually explore our faith. We do no good work in the world that is not subsequent to and responsive to the work that a creative God is already doing. It's God's world, and God intends to have it back; and to get back the world, God uses ordinary United Methodists, through whom God does some extraordinary work.

The Social Principles

Few United Methodist practices illustrate our practical Christianity more vividly than our Social Principles (which have their roots in the "social creed" of our church, which dates from the early twentieth century). The *Discipline* defines these principles as ***our most recent official summary of stated convictions that seek to apply the Christian vision of righteousness to social, economic, and political issues.*** The God whom United Methodists worship combines love with justice, is not only gracious but also demanding, and not only died for you and me but for the whole world. There is for us no personal gospel *that fails to express itself in relevant social concerns; we proclaim no* social gospel *that does not include personal transformation of sinners.*

The Social Principles are a thoughtful effort on the part of a succession of General Conferences to speak to the pressing human issues in the contemporary world from a Wesleyan biblical and theological foundation. They are intended to be instructive; to teach contemporary United Methodists the best thought and practice on selected subjects; and also to be persuasive, urging the church on to higher righteousness. The Social Principles call all members of the United Methodist Church to a prayerful, studied examination of our life together and our personal lives in the light of the gospel.

Our struggles for human dignity and social reform have been a response to God's demand for love, mercy, and justice in the light of the Kingdom. We proclaim no* personal gospel *that fails to express itself in relevant social concerns; we proclaim no* social gospel *that does not include the personal transformation of sinners.

The Social Principles begin by addressing issues in "The Natural World"—ecological concerns, energy resources, technology, and space exploration. They then address "The Nurturing Community," beginning with the family, moving to marriage (we're in favor of it), and then divorce (we're against it but recognize that it sometimes is a "regrettable alternative in the midst of brokenness"). There is a discussion of homosexuality (an argument that has consumed much time and attention in recent meetings of the General Conference), as well as a long paragraph on abortion (I suspect that this paragraph is trying to please everybody by saying next to nothing). "The Social Community" section is dominated by the language of "rights"—rights of children, young people, the aging, and persons with disabilities. I find it hard to square this language of "rights" (which comes from our republican form of government) with either the biblical or the Wesleyan stress on grace and life as gift, but this section is one of the longest in the Social Principles. There are also extensive discussions on "The Economic Community," "The Political Community" (the person who said that the church ought to "stick to saving souls and stay out of politics" wasn't a United Methodist!), and "The World Community." We have churchly opinions on just about everything.

Frankly, some of these sections show the challenge of asserting the primacy of Scripture and at the same time attempting to speak on many topics for which Scripture has no apparent concern. The theological underpinnings of our social teachings are not always clear. Even though these principles are our collective wisdom on social, public, political matters, the *Discipline's* scant attention to personal, individual sin when compared with this extensive and detailed treatment of social sin is odd. Wesley certainly held the personal and the social together. But we live in a curious age in which, if we think of sin at all, we focus more on the sins of Congress or the corporate board room than sins committed by individuals in a bedroom. Sometimes it's safer to love a whole neighborhood than to love our individual neighbors. It's always sad when we United Methodists show our conformity to the world rather than God's calls to help transform the world. In the great Wesleyan tradition, there is no clear demarcation between the personal and the corporate, the social and the individual. The light of Christ penetrates every somber corner of our lives, personal and corporate, and we are under obligation as followers of Christ to let that light shine.

> Religion that is pure and undefiled before God, the Father, is this: to care for the orphans and widows in their distress, and to keep oneself unstained by the world. (Jas. 1:27)

Today United Methodists have over 80 hospitals, 64 extensive child-care networks, and 214 retirement communities and nursing homes for the elderly. We have over a hundred colleges and universities in the United States and about the same number elsewhere.

United Methodist agencies like UMCOR are first on the scene of disaster and calamity with emergency aid and relief. All of this is the institutional result of our Wesleyan theological commitments to faith and good works. (John Wesley not only dispensed theology but also claims to have dispensed medicine to over five hundred persons in London each week.) The term "organized religion" is not to us an insult. We believe that love is less than fully incarnational when it fails to organize and institutionalize.

In Mark's Gospel Jesus is confronted by a rich young man who asks a theological question (Mark 10:17–22) about the inheritance of "eternal life." Jesus responds to the man's question by urging him to obey "the commandments." When the young man says that he has obeyed all the commandments, Jesus adds yet another, telling him to "go, sell what you have, and give to the poor, and you will have treasure in heaven." Maybe it would take a Wesleyan to notice, but did you note that Jesus responds to a rather theoretical, theological question with ethics? Jesus somehow connects "eternal life" with obedience—"go . . . sell . . . give to the poor"?

It is our conviction that the good news of the Kingdom must judge, redeem, and reform the sinful social structures of our time.

So if you thought this excursion into United Methodist beliefs was going to be a comfortable, detached, discussion of great ideas, forget it. We're not talking the distinctively United Methodist way of believing if we're not talking practical, embodied, obedient Christianity. Randy Maddox called my attention to an exchange of letters that Wesley had with a Miss J. C. March, who had written to Wesley about some inadequacies in her spiritual life, especially her difficulty visiting the poor. Wesley wrote to Miss March, without apparent sympathy for her plight, and urged her to give up her gentlewoman status and to seek the higher status of a disciple of Jesus. How? "Go see the poor and sick in their own poor little hovels. Take up your cross, woman! Remember the faith! Jesus went before you, and will go with you. Put off the gentlewoman; you bear an higher character. You are an heir of God!"[5]

And in a letter to her about two years later, in response to her continued complaints about her difficulty in visiting the poor, an aggravated Wesley replied, "I find time to visit the sick and the poor; and I must do it, if I believe the Bible. . . . I am concerned for you; I am sorry you should be content with lower degrees of usefulness and holiness than you are called to." Wesley generally believed that there wasn't much wrong with our relationship with Jesus Christ that couldn't be cured by getting busy in Christ's work, going where Christ goes, doing what Christ commands us.

Faith Known by Its Fruits

The communal forms of faith in the Wesleyan tradition not only promote personal growth, they also equip and mobilize us for mission and service to the world.

Fully a fourth of Wesley's sermons focus on the Sermon on the Mount. Wesley took with great seriousness the Sermon on the Mount as a practical guide to how to live the Christian life. That's curious because most of us today think of Jesus' exhortations in the Sermon on the Mount—turning the other cheek, not remarrying after divorce, enemy love—to be utterly impossible ideals. Wesley gave thanks that Jesus so simply, directly gave us practical guidance for everyday discipleship. He said that the Beatitudes were a picture of God drawn by God's own hand.[6] These commands are not meant to frustrate us forever by their impossibility, said Wesley, but are meant to be actually practiced with the help of God. When faced with some seemingly impossible demand of Christ—such as forgiveness of our enemies—we are to change the church and ourselves rather than attempt to scale down the command.

In our church's recent debate on the U.S. invasion of Iraq, I was impressed how infrequently anyone referred to Jesus. And when someone mentioned Jesus, most disputants seem to agree that Jesus is irrelevant to a contemporary conflict like the "War on Terror." We had made Jesus' command to love the enemy into an impossible ideal. This is distressingly "unmethodist."

We Wesleyans once assumed that Jesus himself combined personal righteousness with social holiness, that his ethic is not to be relegated to the personal and the subjective, the ideal and the unrealistic, but is meant to go public and be put into practice. Jesus came to teach us about the "real world," and we are called to follow him there out of the fake world where the poor are oppressed, the strong lord over the weak, and, well, you get the point. Our United Methodist Social Principles are an attempt to render the real world in the light of the love of Christ.

Early Methodists contended that the urge to holiness in thought and life can be perverted when holiness is not linked to love. Love is not sentimental syrup that we pour over everything to make our problems easier to swallow. Love is the complex, multifaceted force that drives us to engage in the world's needs in the name of Christ. Love is the divine gift that enables true moral transformation. How sad when contemporary United Methodists attempt to scale down the dominical demand for love to the secular political possibility of justice. It is also sad to see contemporary United Methodists choosing up sides on the political left or the right and slugging it out in political squabbles that Wesley would surely dismiss as debates about mere "opinions." Too many of us are confident that being on the "right side" of some social or political issue is more important than being there in love.

It is a constant challenge for us to think and to live on the basis of our theological convictions. Wesley cared as much for our being and our believing as for our doing. Christians are meant to serve the needs of others, in love. The notion of "Christian perfection" can be an ugly thing if not always answerable to love. And the practice of politically engaged social Christianity degenerates into just another worldly power play when it is loveless. Jesus didn't call us simply to improve our neighbors but to love them as he has loved us.

Note that we use that word *discipline* when we talk of social ethics. United Methodists use *discipline* as both a verb and a noun.[7] Discipline in the sense of a *Book of Discipline* is constitutive of church governance. For us, discipleship and discipline go together. In a sermon on "The Late Work of God in North America," Wesley said that the great limitation of the evangelistic ministry of George Whitefield was lack of discipline:

> [I]t was a true saying, which was common in the ancient church, "The soul and the body make a man, and the spirit and discipline make a Christian." But those who were more or less affected by

Mr. Whitefield's preaching had no discipline at all. They had no shadow of discipline; nothing of the kind. They were formed into no societies. They had no Christian connection with each other, nor were ever taught to watch over each others' souls. So that if any fell into lukewarmness, or even into sin, he had none to lift him up. . . .[8]

Holiness and discipline go together:

Prepare your minds for action; discipline yourselves; set all your hope on the grace that Jesus Christ will bring you when he is revealed. Like obedient children, do not be conformed to the desires that you formerly had in ignorance. Instead, as he who called you is holy, be holy yourselves, in all your conduct; for it is written, "You shall be holy, for I am holy." (1 Pet. 1:13–16)

The Social Principles, along with our General Rules, are testimony to the continuing role of disciplined holiness—personal and social holiness—in the United Methodist way of being Christian. Our church attempts to be more than simply an expression of the religious yearnings of its members. In these principles, guides, and rules, the church seeks to conform us, change us, and discipline us to the nature of Christ. As Wesley summarized the message that he expected his traveling preachers to proclaim: "Christ dying for us" *and* "Christ reigning in us."[9]

No motif in the Wesleyan tradition has been more consistent than the link between Christian doctrine and Christian living. Methodists have always been strictly enjoined to maintain the unity of faith and good works, through the means of grace. . . . The coherence of faith with ministries of love forms the discipline of Wesleyan spirituality and Christian discipleship. . . . Discipline was not church law; it was a way of discipleship.

Any truly Wesleyan vision of the Christian life includes direct, personal, sacrificial encounter with suffering persons—simply collecting money for someone else to work with the poor is not enough. Also, Wesley stressed a need for understanding the root causes of poverty. He avoided the typical moral explanations for poverty that were in vogue in his day (and our day too). Wesley also didn't mind urging governmental officials to do their part in response to human need. Why does the United Methodist General Board of Church and Society lobby Congress? Not simply from a desire for a better functioning society but rather from our theological vision of God, whose presence and love among us is always "good news to the poor," and our passionate desire to walk with this God.

Wealth, which Wesley regarded with high suspicion, needed three rules to keep greed in check: *Gain all you can, save all you can, and give all you can.* Here is the summation of one of Wesley's diatribes against wealth:

> Heathen custom is nothing to us. We follow no men any farther than they are followers of Christ. Hear ye him. Yea, today, while it is called today, hear and obey his voice. At this hour and from this hour do his will; fulfill his word in this and in all things. I entreat you, in the name of the Lord Jesus, act up to the dignity of your calling. No more sloth! Whatsoever your hand findeth to do, do it with your might. No more waste! Cut off every expense which fashion, caprice, or flesh and blood demand. No more covetousness! But employ whatever God has entrusted you with in doing good, all possible good, in every possible kind and degree, to the household of faith, to all men.[10]

Wesley's 1739 decision to go out and preach in the fields to the masses and engage in the innovative practice of "field preaching" in the open air was his dramatic attempt to take the gospel to England's new urban poor, just as he had worked among the poor at Oxford for a decade before. He defined the gospel as "good news to the poor" (Luke 4). Right up to the very end of his life, John Wesley worked to set right what was wrong with the world, supporting the Strangers' Friend Society to help newcomers to England's great cities. He worked to end the scourge of slavery, as in his famous last letter to William Wilberforce in 1791. Just four years before his death, he welcomed Sarah Mallet as a preacher— the first officially sanctioned female preacher of Methodism. He gave away all that he made from his books and writings, dying a pauper. Six poor men bore Wesley's body to its grave.

We see God's grace and human activity working together in the relationship of faith and good works. God's grace calls forth human response and discipline.

8

We Believe in the Coming of God's Realm and Reign to the World

We pray and work for the coming of God's realm and reign to the world and rejoice in the promise of everlasting life that overcomes death and the forces of evil.

This book, like everything (except the love of God in Christ), is coming to an end. It's time for end talk. That's what the Christian word "eschatology" means—talk about the end. United Methodists consider that our life in the church is preparation for and a foretaste of the end. In daily speech, we use that phrase "the end" in at least two ways. The word *end* means "final"—the end of the game, the last chapter of the book, the ultimate ticktock of time. The end in this sense is when it is all over and done with, *finis.*

In another sense, *end* also means "purpose"—the result of the work, the meaning of the movie, the point of it all. "End," in this sense, means how it all finally adds up, where it all eventually leads, *telos.* An early Protestant catechism asked, "What is the chief end of humanity?" to which the new Christian exuberantly answered, "To glorify God and to enjoy God forever." Our purpose, our end, is for no more utilitarian reason that the glorification and enjoyment of God. We were made, body and soul, for praise.

To be sure, we shall end. Nothing about us goes on forever. Plato taught that we have an immortal soul, an inextinguishable spark within. Though most Americans seem to believe just that, United Methodists don't. You can write over the lives of your wisest and most noble women and men, the years of youthful exuberance, our greatest human achievements and grandest attainments, *This too shall pass.*

Here's a psalm we often read at funerals:

> You turn us back to dust,
>   and say, "Turn back, you mortals."
> . . . .
> You sweep them away; they are like a dream,
>   like grass that is renewed in the morning;
> in the morning it flourishes and is renewed;
>   in the evening it fades and withers.
>
> (Ps. 90:3, 5–6)

Scripture tells us the truth: no nation, no institution (including the United Methodist Church!), no person goes on forever. Work out at the gym, eat oat bran and wild rice until you pop, you will still, in the end, be a corpse. We are finite. Everything always ends at a cemetery. To know that we are mortal, bounded and finite; to see that this world—as stable as it may seem at the moment—is passing, this is wisdom. Surely this is what the psalmist means by "Teach us to count our days that we may gain a wise heart" (Ps. 90:12).

But we just can't bear to live within the limits. Unwilling to be finite, we crave the infinite. How can creatures so wonderful as we be content with mortality? Just eat this food, only believe this set of principles, follow this regimen twice daily, take this pill, give your life to this ideal, work hard for this boss, endow this institution—you will live forever. The satanic promise to Adam and Eve in the garden of Eden ("You will be like God") is the lie of immortality. One of the major tasks of Christian theology is to unmask our idols, and the promise of most false gods is godlike imperishability.

Wherein is our hope? Christians are enabled to be so brutally honest about the lethal human situation, so pessimistic about prospects for ultimate human betterment, because we are so honestly optimistic about the power of God in Christ. We stand confident in *the promise of everlasting life that overcomes death and the forces of evil.* Much of what we mean when we say "God" is ultimate vitality, eternal life, that state of being where something's always and forever happening because God is life. If we hope to have life anywhere beyond the limits of this passing life, then we must somehow hitch on to God's eternal life.

We believe that Jesus was not only raised from the dead but also, in an amazing act of love, reaches out and takes us along for the ride. Determined not to defeat death alone, God raises us up for the mutual enjoyment of eternity. As John Calvin put it, "Christ rose again that he might have us as companions in the life to come."[1] This is what we mean by "eternal life"—to be welcomed by God into God's existence, to be subsumed into God's story, to have a place in God's reign. And whenever God does that, then that is eternal life. Here. Now. This is why God made us in the first place and what God has in store for us in the end.

Today, as the world seems to shake on its foundations and the future of our civilization is imperiled, many are curious about the end. Yet those spurious *Left Behind* books were not written by a Wesleyan. We've never been much on speculation about *how* or *when* the world shall end, hearing Jesus say, "About that day and hour no one knows" (Matt. 24:36). We take the words of the risen Christ seriously: "It is not for you to know the times or the periods that the Father has set by his own authority"(Acts 1:7). At our best, we've tried to fix our attention on the hopeful things of Christ here, now, and leave tomorrow in the hands of a God who is not only the Alpha but the Omega too.

But that doesn't mean that we Wesleyans believe nothing about the end—the end as point and purpose rather than as finality. The Christian church begins in a cemetery, in God's great surprise move on death in the resurrection of the body of the crucified Jesus. The book of Revelation comes at the end of the Bible and the beginning of the church. Revelation seems to be the vision of a person whose world was coming apart, whose horizon was bleak. It is a book of strange, even disturbing images and blood and battle and much pain. Yet as so often happens in Scripture, St. John turns the pain into an occasion for hopeful singing and celebration. St. John the Divine poetically says to a persecuted, struggling church: When our trials and tribulations are over, we will find in resurrection that it has been worth the effort and we will know the One who has led the way. The Lamb—the slaughtered, crucified and bloody Lamb—will be positioned at the center of heaven, ruling from a throne.

> Then I saw a new heaven and a new earth; for the first heaven and the first earth had passed away, and the sea was no more. And I saw the holy city, the new Jerusalem, coming down out of heaven from God, prepared as a bride adorned for her husband. And I heard a loud voice from the throne saying,
>
>> "See, the home of God is among mortals.
>> He will dwell with them;
>> they will be his peoples,
>> and God himself will be with them;
>> he will wipe every tear from their eyes,
>> Death will be no more;
>> mourning and crying and pain will be no more,
>> for the first things have passed away."
>
> And the one who was seated on the throne said, "See, I am making all things new." (Rev. 21:1–5)

It's a poetic, visionary celebration of the theological claim—God has triumphed. God has at last got what God wants when "every knee should bend, . . . and every tongue should confess that Jesus Christ is Lord" (Phil. 2:10–11). Jesus shall not only return, triumph, and be revealed; he shall reign. And what about us? The glorification and enjoyment of God, for which we were created, which has been only a momentary and episodic pastime here, shall there be our fulltime job. We shall forever whoop it up in the choir (see Rev. 19).

The philosopher Søren Kierkegaard went about the streets of Copenhagen asking people if they really believed that Jesus was raised from the dead. Almost everyone did. Then he asked them what difference that belief made in the way they went about their business. Kierkegaard concluded that it had not the slightest import.

Though Kierkegaard was a Lutheran, his was a very Methodist sort of question. As we have said earlier, we are not only interested in the orthodoxy of beliefs but also in their practical force. What difference does the resurrection make?

We also look to the end time in which God's work will be fulfilled. This prospect gives us hope in our present actions as individuals and as the Church. This expectation saves us from resignation and motivates our continuing witness and service.

Judgment

Curiously, I find little about Jesus the returning judge or divine judgment in the *Discipline.* I'm not sure why the *Discipline* seems squeamish on this subject; John Wesley sure wasn't. Have we not noted that the Wesleyan tradition emphasizes God's transforming love that makes us coworkers in God's reign? God creates us not only to receive salvation but to participate in it by giving us responsibility.

Judgment is linked to reign. The One on the throne is not only the royal ruler of the world but also righteous judge. That's one reason that in the Apostles' Creed we say that Christ is "seated at the right hand of God the Father Almighty from whence he shall come to judge the quick and the dead."

When we celebrate Communion, we join in the acclamation "Christ has died, Christ has risen, Christ will come again!" According to Scripture, everyone will be resurrected (Rom. 14:10); all will be assembled before the righteous gaze of God; then will come the judgment:

"For all of us must appear before the judgment seat of Christ, so that each may receive recompense for what has been done in the body, whether good or evil. . . . We ourselves are well known to God" (2 Cor. 5:10–11).

God gives us response-ability. The God who gives us life also gives us the freedom and the means to be stewards of our lives. Jesus told many parables about masters who gave gifts to their servants, then went away, telling the servants, "Enjoy the talents, use them." And then the master returns, and then comes the judgment as the master asks simply, "What have you done with what you have been given?" (Matt. 25:14–30). Wesley loved that parable of the Talents, noting that the master is particularly tough on the little one-talent servant, casting him into "outer darkness" (25:30).

"What had he done?" Wesley asks in his commentary on this passage. "He is pronounced wicked, because he was a slothful, unprofitable servant," says Wesley. (And you can imagine with what contempt Wesley held the sin of sloth!) Wesley sneers, "Mere harmlessness, on which many build their hope of salvation, was the cause of his damnation."[2]

As Christians, we are accountable to a higher standard of judgment than the conventional "I do try to live a good life and to help other people when I can" or the dubious "I do what seems right to me." We shall be judged by the Master who expects more of us than mere harmlessness.

That we who live in a society that has a problem with personal responsibility and accountability shall be judged by God may seem harsh. I'll admit that I do not find it a pleasant prospect that one day I shall stand before God, made to look honestly at all that I've been given, then to render account. Whether God shall eternally punish me for what I've done and not done; for what I've said and left unsaid; and for all my sin in thought, word, and deed, I expect that it will be punishment enough to be in the presence of divine love and to realize how I have time and again thwarted that love. God's justice shall not be forever mocked. This is the bad news of judgment.

Yet there is also good news—gospel in the notion of a final "day of judgment." In Matthew's account of the Great Judgment (Matt. 31–46), who sits on the throne? The Judge who shall hold us accountable and who shall punish the wicked and reward the righteous is the Crucified Christ, the one who, in suffering love, came to seek and to save sinners. "God did not send his Son into the world to condemn the world but in order that the world might be saved through him" (John 3:17).

The Judge is also the King. Christ did not merely set up laws for our guidance and offer principles for our betterment; he came to us, suffered because of us and with us, and summoned forth "a new people in water and the Spirit," as we say in our baptismal service. In the end, we believe things will not only be accounted for and judged but also set right. For those of us who are blessed with good health, loving families, enough to eat, enough to spend, good jobs, and bright futures, it is natural for us not to think much about a final reckoning. As Jesus once said, we have our reward (Matt. 6:5). But what about the poor child who dies of malnutrition? Or the victim of domestic violence? Or the one whose life is cut short by some illness? The conviction that God is not only compassionate and empathetic but also actively, ultimately, triumphantly just is the hope expressed when we say, "He shall come to judge the quick and the dead." God will right our wrong. God will get God's way, in the end.

Why doesn't God simply "let us be"? Why must God hold us accountable, and why accountable to a standard as high as Christ? We United Methodists believe that God is not only love; God is active, resourceful, transforming, cooperative love. The love of God is not only something that we gaze on from afar, as we look at God's work in Christ's cross and resurrection. God's love is active in us. God expects us to make a difference, holding us accountable for the gifts God has given us.

"When the Son of Man comes in his glory, and all the angels with him, then he will sit on the throne of his glory. All the nations will be gathered before him, and he will separate people one from another as a shepherd separates the sheep from the goats. . . . Then the king will say to those at his right hand, 'Come, you that are blessed by my Father, inherit the kingdom prepared for you from the foundation of the world; for I was hungry and you gave me food, I was thirsty and you gave me something to drink, I was a stranger and you welcomed me, I was naked and you gave me clothing, I was sick and you took care of me, I was in prison and you visited me." (Matt. 25:31–36)

Here's a Wesleyan question: Will God's transformative work in us and God's expectations for us continue, maybe even expand, after our death, in whatever eternity God has in mind for us? The church teaches that everlasting life is a place of blessed, eternal rest, but we Wesleyans are not big on rest. Perhaps God will continue working with us, transforming us, refashioning us into a more perfected image of God's glory. Wesley hints that even heaven may be place for growth in grace.[3] Who knows?

Eternal Life

We also look to the end time in which God's work will be fulfilled. This prospect gives us hope in our present actions as individuals and as the Church. This expectation saves us from resignation and motivates our continuing witness and service.

"Eternal life," "everlasting life," or "heaven" are synonyms for that time, that place, that confluence of events whereby God gets what God wants. A reticence to speak about such matters may be due more to our present economic circumstances than our modern, progressive worldview. People in power or people who are reasonably well fixed tend not to expect much of God. Again, as Jesus said, we have our reward. Our lives could only be made more difficult by a God who in some future shall ask, "What have you done with what you have been given?"—especially if that happens to be a God who loves the poor and holds the rich to account!

But other people, the sort of people whom the old Methodists once treasured and to whom they felt an obligation—those on the bottom, the powerless, and the miserably futured—if there is not a God who actively rights wrongs and works justice and holds to account, then they are without hope. Modern notions of progress, naïve ideas of innate human goodness, and smug complacency about the present order wilt in the face of true tragedy and deep, systemic, eradicable injustice. That's one reason why we United Methodists think it important for every church to be engaged in ministry to and with the poor and the dispossessed. Wesley taught (I count eighty-six references) that there wasn't much wrong with any Christian, rich or poor, that couldn't be cured by more regular visits to those who were sick or in prison. Such ministry rubs our noses in the need of the world and confronts us with our responsibility in Christ. Wesley taught that all Christians have a responsibility to help those in circumstances worse than theirs, that the poor can be empowered to love others who need them, and that the rich could experience the grace of God when they did something good with their wealth.

In his commentary on Jesus' "The poor you shall always have with you" (Matt. 26:11), Wesley exclaims, "Such is the wise and gracious providence of God that we may have always opportunities of relieving their needs and so laying up for ourselves treasures in heaven."[4]

To be honest, many churches in mainline Protestantism in the United States (including too many United Methodist churches) can be unhappy places these days of membership decline and malaise. We console ourselves by saying, "Every church is losing members" and "Nobody around here is religious anymore." We resign ourselves to slow death by attrition; we deny the decay; and we plaster over the cracks in the wall. You would think, to watch this sort of morbidity, that we lied when we stood and said with the Creed, "I believe . . . in the resurrection of the body and the life everlasting," making a mockery of Easter.

With other Christians we recognize that the reign of God is both a present and future reality. The church is called to be that place where the first signs of the reign of God are identified and acknowledged in the world. Wherever persons are being made new creatures in Christ, wherever the insights and resources of the gospel are brought to bear on the life of the world, God's reign is already effective in its healing and renewing power.

When I begin to read a book (except for detective novels), I usually read the last chapter first. If you know where the author is headed, you will be better able to appreciate how the author gets you there. Knowing the conclusion of the drama, the ultimate end, *gives us hope in our present actions as individuals and as the Church. This expectation saves us from resignation and motivates our continuing witness and service.*

Hope for the end empowers us now. When I asked the director of an inner-city United Methodist mission how on earth he kept going against all odds, working for thirty years among the city's poorest of the poor, he replied, "How on earth? Because I know who will finally win the war. God is not forever mocked. There's a kingdom being prepared there for those who've had next to nothing here, on earth, and I'm eager to show them what it looks like."

I can't think of any food pantry for the poor or shelter for the homeless that's been initiated by a group of secular-Nietzchean-rationalist-postmodernists, though just about every United

Methodist church participates in such ministry. Our eschatology, our faith in the ultimate triumph of God, drives us to participation in a new heaven and a new earth right now. We believe that when Jesus said, " 'I came that they may have life' " (John 10:10) he meant both now and then, here and there, his will done on earth as it is in heaven. Mark says that Jesus' first sermon began with the announcement " 'The time is fulfilled, and the kingdom of God has come near; repent, and believe the good news' " (Mark 1:15). Because we know and expect that time, that place when " 'the kingdom of the world has become the kingdom of our Lord / and of his Messiah, / and he will reign forever and ever" (Rev. 11:15), we do not lose hope. Salvation is the name for our adoption into that kingdom without end: "You are no longer strangers and aliens, but you are citizens with the saints and also members of the household of God" (Eph. 2:19). Affirmation of God's triumph, of the gift of eternal life, of a final judgment for all—these are among the most politically charged and economically relevant of Christian doctrines.

As conversionist, transformationist, sanctificationist Christians, United Methodists—having experienced God's dramatic transformation in our own lives—think it not too much of a leap to imagine God's transformation, sanctification, and conversion of the whole cosmos. The person who said to me after her experience of personal conversion, "It's like the old me is over and there's a whole new me" is just the sort of person who thinks it conceivable that God could do that to the whole creation. Just as in my baptism, the old has been and is being put to death, so in our baptism, a new me is being raised for new life in Christ. Church is a lifetime of dress rehearsal for the move that God will make in us and in all creation in eternal life.

We believe that Jesus defeated death, triumphed, and, in an amazing act of grace, intends to take us along with him through this veil of tears, this life in the present world—all the way to whatever realm awaits in eternity. And we believe this not on some naïve wish for the future but on the solid evidence of his love as we have experienced it here and now. Because God in Christ has gone to such extraordinary lengths to get to us in this life, we cannot believe that God will not continue to reach out to us in death.

There is therefore now no condemnation for those who are in Christ Jesus. . . . If God is for us, who is against us? He who did not withhold his own Son, but gave him up for all of us, will he not with him also give us everything else? . . . Who will separate us from the love of Christ? Will hardship, or distress, or persecution, or famine, or nakedness, or peril, or sword? . . . No, in all these things we are more than conquerors through him who loved us. For I am convinced that neither death, nor life, nor angels, nor rulers, nor things present, nor things to come, nor powers, nor height, nor depth, nor anything else in all creation, will be able to separate us from the love of God in Christ Jesus our Lord. (Rom. 8:1, 31–32, 35, 37–39)[5]

When it comes to anyone's ultimate destiny, our fates are in the hand of a merciful God who is God of the just and the unjust, who makes his sun to shine upon the undeserving heads of both the righteous and the unrighteous (Matt. 5:45).[6] In his mature thought, Wesley seems to have a wider hope for those who do not know Christ.[7] Though to be sure, even when those who do not apparently know Christ are saved, brought into eternal life, this also is through Christ since, as we noted earlier, *any* human response to God is possible only because of the resourceful grace of God that works in us through the saving work of Christ—even when we don't know it. Wesley really believed that God will get what God wants and, in Scripture and in his experience with the people called Methodist, it is clear that God wants the world.[8]

The church is called to be that place where the first signs of the reign of God are identified and acknowledged in the world. Wherever persons are being made new creatures in Christ, wherever the insights and resources of the gospel are brought to bear on the life of the world, God's reign is already effective in its healing and renewing power.

Just after the *Discipline* speaks about "Christ's universal church," it moves immediately to talk about the "coming of God's realm and reign" and "everlasting life." After all, what is the church but an expression of, a foretaste of, and a present experience of eternal life? The church is where we are taught the hope-filled experience of God's eternity now and encouraged to keep taut the tension between the way things are in the kingdom of this world and the way God means for things to be in the kingdom of heaven. We are not permitted to bed down, settle in, and rest content with the injustice, the tragedy, and the limits of this world. The church keeps telling us that there is a new world coming and we are meant to be part of it. Church is where we learn to sing the hopeful first notes of that song that we shall one day sing for all eternity:

> "Hallelujah!
> For the Lord our God
>   the Almighty reigns.
> Let us rejoice and exult
>   and give him the glory."
>   (Rev. 19:6–7)

What we only experience here and there, on Sundays, as special and extraordinary in our life together in the church shall one day be as typical as Monday. Our occasional celebrations of the Lord's Supper or Holy Communion shall be our normal fare as we feast forever at the banquet of the Lord. We shall, in the words of Charles Wesley's hymn, be "lost in wonder, love, and praise." Our social pronouncements condemning present evils shall be vindicated in the new world order that is God's final act of grace. Church is practice for eternal life.

The night before a racist assassin's bullet brought his life to an end, Martin Luther King Jr. preached to the Memphis garbage workers. In his sermon he said,

It's all right to talk about long robes over yonder, in all of its symbolism, but ultimately people want some suits and dresses and shoes to wear down here. It's all right to talk about streets flowing with milk and honey, but God has commanded us to be concerned about the slums down here, and his children who can't eat three square meals a day. It's all right to talk about the new Jerusalem, but one day, God's preacher must talk about the new New York, the new Atlanta, the new Philadelphia, the new Los Angeles, the new Memphis.[9]

The book of Revelation, at the end of the Bible, says that in paradise, when the kingdom of heaven is come in its fullness, there will be no church (Rev. 21:22), not even a United Methodist church. Why? Presumably we won't need church to train us to be in peace with God and our neighbors. We won't have to content ourselves with glimpses of eternity. We will have arrived. The people of God shall shine like the sun. We shall see God not as through a mirror dimly, but face to face (1 Cor. 13:12). We shall know. The veil of mortality shall be lifted. That stunning, glorious light that is God Almighty and the Lamb (Rev. 21:22) shall effusively shine upon us. We shall then fully see God and ourselves as we have been created from the beginning to be. Perfected, washed, and raised, at the end we shall be home.

9

Thinking like Wesleyans

Theology is thinking that takes the loving self-revelation of the living God seriously. *Doctrine* and *beliefs* are what the church has made of the most interesting and persistent aspects of God's revelation. This book has been part of your training as a Christian theologian, that is, training for thinking like a Christian. You have learned of United Methodism's constant linkage of Christian thinking and Christian formation; theological reflection's goal is greater and more truthful self-understanding, transformed lives and practical service, worship in word and deed in the name of Christ.

When John Wesley delineated his "practical divinity" in a 1742 essay, "The Character of a Methodist,"[1] he affirmed, "The distinguishing marks of a Methodist are not his opinions of any sort." (Wesley relegated those theological doctrines that were not primary to "opinions" on which Christians of good will could disagree and still be in communion with one another.) He then asked, "What then is the mark? Who is a Methodist?" and answered, "A Methodist is one who has 'the love of God shed abroad in his heart by the Holy Ghost.'" The test of the validity of a theology, in the light of Christ, is the test of love.

Wesley then continued with a number of "marks" that are derived from Scripture:

> He is therefore happy in God. . . . Having found "redemption through his blood, the forgiveness of his sins," he cannot but rejoice. . . . He rejoiceth also, whenever he looks forward, "in hope of the glory that shall be revealed."

From him, therefore he cheerfully receives all, saying, "Good is the will of the Lord"; . . . For he hath "learned, in whatsoever state he is, therewith to be content."

[H]e "prays without ceasing."

[T]his commandment is written in his heart, that "he who loveth God, loves his brother also."

[H]e is "pure in heart."

[T]he one design of his life is . . . "not to do his own will, but the will of Him that sent him."

[A]s he loves God, so "he keeps his commandments."

[L]oving God with all his heart, he serves him with all his strength. . . . All the talents he has received, he constantly employs according to his Master's will. . . .

[W]hatsoever he doeth, it is all to the glory of God.

Nor do the customs of the world at all hinder his "running the race that is set before him."

Lastly, as he has time, he "does good unto all men"—unto neighbours and strangers, friends and enemies. And that in every possible kind.

These are the *principles* and *practices* of our SECT; these are the *marks* of a true Methodist. . . . By these *marks*, by these fruits of a living faith, do we labour to *distinguish* ourselves from the unbelieving world, from all those whose minds or lives are not according to the gospel of Christ.[2]

To aid in the character formation of Methodists, Wesley published the fifty-volume *A Christian Library: Extracts and Abridgements* between 1749 and 1755. Over his lifetime he published over four hundred items, making available the best of Christian thought for Methodists. Thus the *Discipline's* discussion of "Our Theological Task" ends with the following:

In this spirit we take up our theological task. We endeavor through the power of the Holy Spirit to understand the love of God given in Jesus Christ. We seek to spread this love abroad. As we see more clearly who we have been, as we understand more fully the needs of the world, as we draw more effectively upon our theological heritage, we will become better equipped to fulfill our calling as the people of God.

Theology as Gift of God

None of our thoughts about God is self-generated, thanks to Scripture and the saints. The purpose of United Methodist doctrine is Christian discipleship, a person changed by encounter with Christ, religion of the heart constantly formed and reformed by engagement of the mind that results in hands dedicated to working with Christ.

We know God only because God has communicated with us as the Trinity—Father, Son, and Holy Spirit. In love God has graciously given to us true and reliable, life-giving knowledge of God in order that we might truly love and serve God. That's why all theology, including the theology in this book, is a form of prayer in which we receptively hold out empty hands asking God to give us what we cannot have exclusively by our own effort. For any of us to say, "I believe" is to gratefully acknowledge that God has spoken to us, has revealed to us a truthful way to walk, and has given us that which we did not, in our sin, deserve.

Our beliefs arise out of our convictions about who God is. United Methodist believing is characterized by these distinctive trajectories[3]:

1. *God is actively, relentlessly, fully love.* That's why love, more than justice, hospitality, aid to the poor, or any other noble virtue is at the heart of John Wesley's ethics. God has created us, commanded us, and enabled us to love. Wesley loved both the poor and the rich in the name of Christ and charged both rich and poor with the responsibility to love those in need. Aspirations to holiness or righteousness could become perverted without love. In our life together, in our debates and arguments as a church, we

are enjoined to love both our neighbors and our enemies.[4] As William Abraham shows, Wesley considered God's mercy to be more fundamental than even God's fairness. God is "a God of unblemished justice and truth: but above all is his mercy."[5] Love is God's "reigning attribute, the attribute that sheds an amiable glory on all his other perfections."[6] And to those of us who are such eager beavers to learn, to read books, and to know all we can about God, Wesley said that "without love, all knowledge is but splendid ignorance."

2. *The statement "God is love" has practical implications.* Wesley linked God's sovereignty to God's love. As William Abraham says, Wesley thought of God's power or sovereignty in terms of *empowerment* rather than control or *overpowerment.* God works "strongly and sweetly."[7] God's *grace* works powerfully, but not irresistibly, in human life and salvation, thereby empowering our *response-ability* without overriding our *responsibility.* There is, in Wesley's thought and in the thinking of Wesley's heirs an abiding, life-giving tension: devoid of God's grace, we *cannot* be saved; without our (grace-empowered but uncoerced) involvement, God's grace *does not* save. This is the dynamic sense of Christian life that Randy Maddox designates as "responsible grace,"[8] an interplay between the loving work of God in us and the work of God through us.

3. *God expects not only to be loved but also obeyed* by practice of the faith in disciplined communities of faith. In contemporary theological circles, there is much interest in the recovery of Christian "practice." Discipleship is too difficult and survival as a Christian is too demanding without habitual, formed, and formal practices of discipleship. Prayer, Bible study, sacraments, public worship, and the small-group Christian conferencing that we methodical Wesleyans once cultivated with enthusiasm may be taken up again as essential to Christian believing. It is no small thing that Wesley's greatest theological work was in his crafting of liturgies, hymns, and sermons—those theological practices that were near to the needs of actual believers in their daily walk with Christ. Any real, deep, spiritual transformation must be cultivated and sustained through good habits. The most important Christian

virtues are too important and too against our natural inclinations to be left to when we feel like doing them.

4. *Christ dies for all so that all might be forgiven and always live for him.* At Aldersgate, 1738, Wesley experienced deep assurance that the explosive power of the Reformation emphasis on justification by faith applied to his own life. There can be no real fruits of faith, no true transformation, without God doing something fundamental about our failure and guilt to love God as we are created to love. God has got to do something about our enslavement to the burden of our past, and in the cross and resurrection of Christ God does. What is done in Jesus Christ is done for everyone, for there are no limits to God's love. Faith is the result of a personal assurance of the significance of Christ's cross and resurrection, given through the work of the Holy Spirit. The Holy Spirit gives confirmation of our relationship with Christ (e.g., Aldersgate); therefore we need not anxiously worry about our status before God.

5. *Love of God results in a lifelong quest to please God by doing godly work.* In the Conference of 1770, Wesley answered his Calvinist critics' charge that he had made salvation into a program of human good work rather than the exclusive work of God in Christ. He defended good works as an essential sign that we're on the path of salvation. By the grace of God, human agency is real. God graciously gives us a role in the process of our salvation.[9] Wesley's unhesitating emphasis on the proffer of God's love to all (universal atonement and prevenient grace) and the liberation and empowerment of all who respond (sanctification and holiness) remains a hallmark of United Methodist believing.

6. *Christ can change everyone whom he calls.* Jesus not only forgives our sins but enables transformed lives. United Methodists are restlessly, vibrantly conversionist and transformationist in our thinking. When we read some biblical text or when we examine a core Christian belief, our question is not simply the abstract and intellectual "Can I believe this?" but the more incarnational "How would my life need to change in order to demonstrate the truth of this claim?" United Methodism is about dramatic change that leads to our active participation in Christ's transformation of the world that is holiness of heart and life. Being a Christian is not synony-

mous with being a thinking, caring American—a Christian is someone who has been changed by Christ to talk more like Christ and to walk more like Christ every moment in life.

7. *Theology in service to a complex and rich Trinitarian God keeps many seemingly opposing beliefs in conversation and tension with one another.* There is tension in United Methodist doctrine as competing notions are paired in order for theology to be as rich, multifaceted, and full as is Jesus Christ. Rationality and emotionalism, Jesuit-like discipline and Pentecostal ecstasy, success in acquisition of wealth and frugality, justification and sanctification, pragmatic functionalism and reflective theologizing, pious innocence and sophisticated learning, democratic volunteerism and hierarchical structure, God's free grace and our hard work—the list of United Methodist antimonies is long and, we believe, full of life-giving theological energy. The much-discussed, sometimes maligned "Wesleyan quadrilateral"—Scripture, tradition, reason, and experience (not a United Methodist doctrine but rather a pattern of thought, a means of interpretation)—enables us to play some essentials of Christian thought in concert with one another.

8. *An appropriate response to the loving generosity of God toward us is a generous, open-handed, ecumenical spirit toward our fellow Christians.* While he worried about the impact of false understandings of God on the Christian formation of his people, and he took great care to distinguish the false from the true when it came to Christian believing, Wesley attempted to be generous in his judgments about the theological positions of others. In a sermon that he delivered upon the death of his friend and critic George Whitefield, Wesley urged,

> Let us keep close to the grand scriptural doctrines which he [Whitefield] everywhere delivered. There are many doctrines of a less essential nature, with regard to which even the sincere children of God (such is the present weakness of human understanding!) are and have been divided for many ages. In these we may think and let think; we may "agree to disagree." But meantime let us hold fast the essentials of "the faith which was once delivered to the saints," and which this champion of God so strongly insisted on at all times and in all places.[10]

Love must be practiced in our believing. In his famous sermon on "The Catholic Spirit," Wesley said,

> A catholic spirit . . . is not an indifference to *all* opinions. This is the spawn of hell. A man of a truly catholic spirit . . . is fixed as the sun in his judgment concerning the main branches of Christian doctrine. Go first and learn the first elements of the gospel of Christ, and then shall you learn to be of a truly catholic spirit. But while he is steadily fixed on his religious principles . . . his heart is enlarged toward all mankind; he embraces with strong and cordial affection neighbors and strangers, friends and enemies. For love alone gives the title to this character: catholic love is a catholic spirit.[11]

Methodist Doctrine is admittedly lean when compared with expansive and detailed Catholic doctrine or the sweeping panorama of Reformed thought. We pray that simplicity is a virtue and that our simple, essentialist approach to Christian believing removes as many barriers as possible from our believing in common with other brothers and sisters in Christ.

Let our last words in this theological journey echo those of John Wesley. As he lay on his deathbed, even as he died, Wesley articulated the most important, absolutely essential, beginning and end of our Christian lives saying, "The best of all is, God is with us."

United Methodist believing—best of all—is a sign and validation that God is with us.

Notes

INTRODUCTION AND WARNING

1. Although I am a United Methodist, I would be surprised if the beliefs that I highlight, and my interpretation of them, would be challenged by the other three main branches of Episcopal Methodism in the United States: African Methodist Episcopal, African Methodist Episcopal Zion, and Christian Methodist Episcopal.

2. It's a mistake to think that people will more willingly embrace the Christian gospel if we can just find a catchy way to repackage it so that they no longer feel an offense. One reason that people have trouble believing in the gospel is that it is a complex of beliefs that are against just about everything they already believe. Theology helps to make those differences and difficulties clear, not simply to do away with them in order to make the gospel more palatable to people without intellectual struggle or the shock of moral transformation.

3. "The Way to the Kingdom," sec. 1.6, in Frank Baker, ed., *The Bicentennial Edition of the Works of John Wesley* (Nashville: Abingdon Press, 1990), 1:220–21.

4. Three able United Methodist theologians aided me in writing this book: Russell Richey, Richard Heitzenrater, and Randy Maddox. I thank them for their invaluable assistance in responding to my presentation of United Methodist theology.

5. In writing this book and in addressing you thus, I am only doing what the church has called me to do. *The Book of Discipline of the United Methodist Church* (Nashville: United Methodist Publishing House, 2004) gives to bishops the task of doctrinal teaching in the whole denomination. In section 4 of chapter 3 of the *Discipline*, "Specific Responsibilities of Bishops," paragraph 414 is labeled "Leadership—Spiritual and Temporal," referring to the Constitution's provision that we bishops be responsible for "the general oversight and promotion of the temporal and spiritual interests of the entire Church." Subparagraph 3 gives bishops the responsibility "to guard, transmit, teach, and proclaim, corporately and individually, the apostolic faith as it is expressed in Scripture and

tradition, and, as they are led and endowed by the Spirit, to interpret that faith evangelically and prophetically." I hope that my quoting of these paragraphs to you gives my work a credence that it might not otherwise have.

6. Lord help you if you picked up this book thinking that it is "Methodist Beliefs for Dummies."

CHAPTER 1: WE BELIEVE IN THE TRIUNE GOD

1. This book on United Methodist beliefs is organized on the basis of selected statements from "Doctrinal Standards and Our Theological Task," part 2 of *The Book of Discipline of the United Methodist Church* (Nashville: United Methodist Publishing House, 2004). The *Discipline*, as we United Methodists call our book of church order and guidance, is the sourcebook for our life together. Alas, most of us think of the *Discipline* as our "book of rules and regulations." True, we're big on rules, and true, the *Discipline* is full of them. But before it gets to any rules and regulations, the *Discipline* is a book of United Methodist beliefs. The first part of the *Discipline*, after our Constitution, is a full discussion of theology. Please note that the word "discipline" is directly related to the word "disciple." Here are the beliefs we need to enable us to follow Jesus rather than some other alleged savior.

Most of the doctrinal paragraphs were written by Richard P. Heitzenrater, working with doctrinal study committees chaired by the Methodist theologian Albert C. Outler (1968–72) and by Bishop Earl Hunt (1984–88) and were approved at the General Conferences of 1972 and 1988.

Get a copy of our *Discipline* and read part 2 for yourself. Our doctrine is the authoritative, official body of teachings of our church regarding what we ought to believe and what we ought to do as Christians. It's what Methodists have agreed we ought to teach as our cherished beliefs. You'll quickly find that it's a libel against us Wesleyans to say, "Methodists believe fairly much anything they want." I will order this book on the basis of the systematic discussion of United Methodist beliefs that is found in the *Discipline*.

2. Sermon 55, "On the Trinity," sec. 17, Frank Baker, ed., *The Bicentennial Edition of the Works of John Wesley* (Nashville: Abingdon Press, 1990), 2:384.

3. Although we have only one published sermon that Wesley devoted to the doctrine, the Trinity crops up frequently in Wesley's actual sermons. He praised his brother Charles's marvelous *Hymns on the Trinity* (1767) and described Christ working in us to make us veritable "Transcripts of the Trinity" (hymn #7, in Baker, *Works*, 7:88). See sermon 55, "On the Trinity," sec. 3, in Baker, *Works*, 2:376–77. Albert Outler notes (in Baker, *Works*, 2:373) twenty-three references to the Trinity in Wesley's preaching.

4. Many praise Wesley for his "catholic spirit," his reaching out to those who differed with him theologically. He drew the line at acceptance of Deists, certain that their views struck a deathblow to the heart of the faith. See sermon 64 in Baker, *Works*, 500–10.

5. You will note, in the above comments, the frequent use of the conjunction "and," an important word for United Methodist theology. We Wesleyans tend to practice what Kenneth Collins has called "conjunctive theology." Early Methodism loved to hold together seemingly contradictory ideas at one time. More than Calvinism, we held together the universal atonement wrought by Christ *and* the need for a personal, life-changing commitment by each person. More than Lutheranism, we held together justification *and* sanctification. More than Puritan antisacramentalism, we held together preaching *and* sacraments, the local congregation *and* the holy catholic church, free church *and* catholic forms of worship. And to Calvinists, Lutherans, and Puritans, we said that we loved them and agreed with them on most that they believed! More than Unitarianism we Trinitarians affirmed "these three are one."

6. Quoted in Albert Outler, ed., *John Wesley* (New York: Oxford University Press, 1964), 66. Note Wesley's italics, denoting that Wesley hereby moved from an idea of salvation to the personal assurance of salvation.

CHAPTER 2: WE BELIEVE IN SALVATION THROUGH JESUS CHRIST

1. Wesley's letter to "Various Clergymen," April 19, 1764, in John Telford, ed., *The Letters of the Rev. John Wesley, A. M.*, 8 vols. (London: Epworth, 1931), 4:237. Most English Christian leaders of Wesley's day—Anglican and Dissenters—thought Wesley's list absurdly short. We present-day Wesleyans think Wesley's doctrinal brevity a virtue.

2. Frank Baker, ed., *The Bicentennial Edition of the Works of John Wesley* (Nashville: Abingdon Press, 1990), 1:586.

3. Baker, *Works,* 1:226–27.

CHAPTER 3: WE BELIEVE IN THE HOLY SPIRIT

1. This implies that if we are not being dragged into court by the cops, so that we don't need the Holy Spirit to represent us, we may not be working with Jesus.

CHAPTER 4: WE BELIEVE IN CHRIST'S UNIVERSAL CHURCH

1. Thomas Coke and Francis Asbury, *The Doctrines and Discipline of the Methodist Episcopal Church in America with Explanatory Notes* (Philadelphia: Henry Tuckniss, 1798; repr. Rutland, VT: Academy Books, 1979), 52.

2. John Wesley, *Journal*, in *Works of John Wesley on Compact Disc*, pt. 3, para. 17.

3. Arminius taught that faith was a gift that was imputed to the sinner for righteousness, whereas earlier Reformed teaching had stressed that faith was mostly a matter of the object of faith, Christ and His righteousness. Arminius shifted the exclusive focus of salvation from God's work in Christ to the synergistic activity of human faith enabled by God's grace. Faith, for Arminius, became a work required of us for salvation, a work that from start to finish is motivated and enabled by God, but still, a good work. Arminius's critics charged that he undermined the Protestant doctrine of justification by faith alone, salvation as complete gift of God. Critics of Wesley's sanctificationism said much the same about Wesley. We contemporary Arminians deny the charge.

4. Sermon 43, "The Scripture Way of Salvation," sec. 3.6, in Frank Baker, ed., *The Bicentennial Edition of the Works of John Wesley* (Nashville: Abingdon Press, 1990), 2:64.

CHAPTER 5: WE BELIEVE IN PRACTICING THEOLOGY

1. We Wesleyans don't have much theology to believe other than that which we sing. Sappy, sentimental songs sung in church can lead to flaccid, superficial disciples in the world. So our main way of enforcing "correct" theological discourse is by urging our folks to sing what's printed in the hymnal.

2. What the Catholics call the "magisterium," the teaching office of the Catholic Church, is located for the United Methodist Church in our General Conference. In 1744 John Wesley convened a group to discuss the state of their Methodist revival. Wesley organized his conferences around three questions: "What to teach; how to teach; and what to do?" Note that the function of teaching, or doctrine, was to move toward practice. When Methodism became an independent denomination in the United States, its conference of preachers was the supreme authority in all matters. Today this tradition continues as the United Methodist Church places its doctrinal authority in the hands of the General Conference, subject to the limits placed upon it by the Restrictive Rules.

3. Jonathan Edwards, *Religious Affections* (1746), ed. John E. Smith (New Haven, CT: Yale University Press, 1959), 411.

4. "Wesleyan quadrilateral" was coined by Albert Outler to point to a process through which Wesley relied more on "standards of doctrine" than on systematic theology or confessions of faith. Anglicans usually talk about three means (Scripture, tradition, and reason). We Wesleyans, not surprisingly, added "experience."

5. Among the slipperiest of terms is "experience" since many today confuse "spirituality" with mere personal experience or equate "revelation" with "experience." It is surprising that so many of us still trust our "experience" after Freud showed us how our experience is so full of various unconscious determinants and after Marx taught us that our experience is formed and limited by our economic location. Wesleyans believe that "experience" is when the Holy Spirit directs us toward the Incarnation of the Son of God.

6. Here is how Albert Outler, editor of Wesley's sermons, sums up Wesley's interpretative principles:
   1. The Scriptures must be read according to their own "general sense."
   2. Since the Scriptures constitute a coherent whole, the clearer texts may be relied upon to illuminate the obscurer one.
   3. The literal sense is to be preferred, unless its irrational or unworthy implications demand that one rather seek for a more edifying spiritual meaning.
   4. All moral commands in Scripture are also "covered promises," since God never commands the impossible and his grace is always efficacious in every faithful will.
   5. The historical experience of the church, though fallible, is the better judge overall of Scripture's meanings than individual interpreters are likely to be (in Frank Baker, ed., *The Bicentennial Edition of the Works of John Wesley* [Nashville: Abingdon Press, 1990], 58f.).

7. *The Book of Discipline of the United Methodist Church* (Nashville: United Methodist Publishing House, 2004), 72.

CHAPTER 6: WE BELIEVE IN TRANSFORMING AND PERFECTING GRACE

1. Sermon 43, "The Scripture Way of Salvation," sec. 1.2, in Frank Baker, ed., *The Bicentennial Edition of the Works of John Wesley* (Nashville: Abingdon Press, 1990), 2:157.

2. Baker, *Works*, 7:323.

3. Sermon 43, "The Scripture Way of Salvation," sec. 1.1, in Baker, *Works*, 2:156.

4. Albert Outler, "Pastoral Care in the Wesleyan Spirit," *Perkins School of Theology Journal* 25 (1971): 10.

5. Letter to Mary Cooke (30 Oct. 1785), as quoted in Randy Maddox, *Responsible Grace, John Wesley's Practical Theology* (Nashville: Abingdon Press, 1994), 156.

6. Maddox, *Responsible Grace*, 19.

7. Baker, *Works* 2:163.

8. *Ibid.,* 1:274; "Witness of the Spirit I" (1.7).

9. John Wesley, *The Principles of a Methodist Further Explained* (1745), in *The Works of John Wesley on Compact Disc* (Franklin, TN: Providence House Publishers, 1995).

10. Lutherans stress that we are, even after justification, fully justified and fully sinful, sinful and saintly at the same time. We don't stop being sinful just because we are justified. In the Reformed tradition (Calvin and his heirs) there is

a constant struggle with sin, and whatever victories we have over sin tend not to last. Wesley tends to agree with both Lutherans and Calvinists on these points yet differs on sanctification—namely, on the idea that God imparts righteousness to converted sinners whereby we actually become holy, being freed from the power as well as the guilt of sin, and having the possibility (though not probability) of living without committing conscious, voluntary, knowing sins (being totally saturated with love of God and neighbor).

11. Sermon 107, "On God's Vineyard," 1787, in Thomas Jackson, ed., *The Works of John Wesley,* 3rd ed. (London: Wesleyan Methodist Book Room, 1872; repr., Grand Rapids, MI: Baker, 1979), 7:202–13, particularly 204.

12. This assertion of the possibility of "backsliding" led to a century of arguments between Methodists and Baptists on the American frontier. The Baptists said "once saved, always saved"; the Methodists worried about backsliding. While critics charged that Methodists made the Christian life into an anxious, never-for-sure matter of constant striving to stay saved, the Methodists responded that sometimes classical Protestantism reduced God's gracious work to a one-time fix that failed to bear fruit in continuing responsiveness in the lives of believers. There is some truth in both sides of the argument, and much unproductive caricature as well.

13. Albert Outler, "The Place of Wesley in the Christian Tradition," in *The Place of John Wesley in the Christian Tradition*, ed. Kenneth E. Rowe (Metuchen, NJ: Scarecrow Press, 1976), 22, italics mine.

14. John Wesley, *Explanatory Notes upon the New Testament* (London: Epworth Press, 1944), 35.

15. John Wesley, *Farther Appeal to Men of Reason and Religion,* pt. 1, para. 3, in *Works of John Wesley on Compact Disc.*

16. The miraculous only became a problem for Christianity when we capitulated to the limitations of the European Enlightenment and its construction of a natural world that is safely sealed from the intrusions of a living, active God. Christians believe that there is no "supernatural" because for those of us who know the scriptural story there is no "natural." It's all creation by an active Creator.

17. When you consider all the factors against it, that you are actually reading this book on theology is a miracle, sort of.

18. Quoted by William J. Abraham, *Wesley for Armchair Theologians* (Louisville, KY: Westminster John Knox Press, 2005), 101.

CHAPTER 7: WE BELIEVE IN FAITH AND GOOD WORKS

1. John Wesley, *Earnest Appeal,* para. 4, in *The Works of John Wesley on Compact Disc* (Franklin, TN: Providence House Publishers, 1995).

2. John Wesley, *Address to the Clergy* (1756), in Thomas Jackson, ed., *The Works of John Wesley,* 3rd ed. (London: Wesleyan Methodist Book Room, 1872; repr., Grand Rapids, MI: Baker, 1979), 10:480-500

3. Sermon 110, "Free Grace," sec. 10–18, (see sec. 11), in Frank Baker, ed., *The Bicentennial Edition of the Works of John Wesley* (Nashville: Abingdon Press, 1990), 3:547–50.

4. Jackson, *Works of John Wesley,* 14:190–8.

5. As quoted by Maddox in a lecture at Duke University on June 26, 2006. A letter dated June 9, 1775, to Miss March is found in John Telford, ed., *The Letters of the Rev. John Wesley, A. M.*, 8 vols. (London: Epworth, 1931), 6:153–54; one dated February 7, 1776, in Telford, *Letters*, 6:206–7

6. Sermon 23, "Sermon on the Mount III," sec. 4, in Baker, *Works*, 1:533. Wesley described the Sermon on the Mount as "the noblest compendium of religion which is to be found even in the oracles of God," in *Journal* (17 Oct. 1771), in Baker, *Works*, 22:293.

7. Beginning in 1784, the *Book of Discipline* swelled from the size of a small pamphlet to what it is today, nearly 800 pages. I wish this meant that we were continuing to discipline ourselves, in the tradition of the early Methodists. Alas, the bulging book is mostly evidence of the ways in which a corporation-like mentality got hold of us. If there's good worth doing, it's worth passing some rule to mandate it. When United Methodist practices and disciplines lose their theological rationale, they become lifeless and cold. That should be our great worry. I for one wish the *Discipline* disciplined itself to the barest of theological essentials. Back in 1792, the title of our book was *The Doctrines and Discipline of the Methodist Episcopal Church in America.* Note the connection, in this older title, of doctrine and discipline.

8. Jackson, *Works of John Wesley*, 3:598.

9. Letter to Charles Wesley (1928 Dec. 1774), in Telford, *Letters*, 6:134.

10. Jackson, *Works of John Wesley,* 2:279.

CHAPTER 8: WE BELIEVE IN THE COMING OF GOD'S REALM AND REIGN TO THE WORLD

1. John Calvin, *Institutes of the Christian Religion*, ed. John T. McNeill, trans. Ford Lewis Battles, LCC (Philadelphia: Westminister Press, 1960), 3.25.3.

2. John Wesley, *Explanatory Notes on the New Testament,* 1754 (Salem, OH: Schmul Publishers, Rare Reprint Specialists, 1976), 83–84.

3. *Further Thoughts Upon Christian Perfection*, Q. 29, in Thomas Jackson, ed., *The Works of John Wesley*, 3rd ed. (London: Wesleyan Methodist Book Room, 1872; repr., Grand Rapids MI: Baker, 1979), 11:426.

4. Wesley, *Explanatory Notes,* 42.

5. In talk of the "ultimate triumph of God," do United Methodists mean that God ultimately triumphs in every life ("universal salvation")? What of those who steadfastly refuse God's gift, who turn their backs on the suffering love of Christ? Wesley hints that the justice and resourceful love of God extend to people who lacked knowledge of Christ through no fault of their own. But

invincible, hard-hearted ignorance on the part of those who knew about Christ would exclude them from the joys of heaven, even as it has excluded them from the joys of life with Christ here on earth. See Jackson, *Works of John Wesley*, 26:198; and Sermon 55, "On the Trinity," in *Works of John Wesley on Compact Disc* (Franklin, TN: Providence House Publishers, 1995).

6. See Sermon 91, "On Charity," sec. 1.3, *Works on Compact Disc*, 3:295–96; Sermon 127, "On the Wedding Garment," sec. 17, *Works on Compact Disc*, 4:147; and Sermon 130, "On Living Without God," sec. 14, *Works on Compact Disc*, 4:174.

7. See Wesley's sermon "The More Excellent Way," in *Works on Compact Disc*.

8. The "universal atonement" that Wesley asserted before Calvinist critics (Christ died for all, not just a few) is not due to his goofy positive attitude about the human spirit (as we have said, Wesley had a robust notion of human depravity) but rather to his own experience of the triumphant grace of God in Christ.

9. Martin Luther King Jr., *A Testament of Hope: The Essential Writings and Speeches of Martin Luther King, Jr.,* ed. James Melvin Washington (San Francisco: HarperSanFrancisco, 1986), 282.

CHAPTER 9: THINKING LIKE WESLEYANS

1. Frank Baker, ed., *The Bicentennial Edition of the Works of John Wesley* (Nashville: Abingdon Press, 1990), vol. 9.

2. Wesley's *Character of a Methodist* in volume 9 of his *Works,* quoted and discussed in Russell E. Richey, *Marks of Methodism: Theology in Ecclesial Practice,* with Dennis M. Campbell and William B. Lawrence (Nashville: Abingdon Press, 2005), 2–3.

3. I am indebted, in many of the following insights, to the delightful work of William J. Abraham, *Wesley for Armchair Theologians* (Louisville, KY: Westminster John Knox Press, 2005), 37–40.

4. In the current acrimonious debates in our church, sometimes it seems as if we find it easier to love the oppressed Palestinians, the unborn, the politically conservative, or the politically liberal (pick your favorite object of love) than we love our fellow United Methodists!

5. Sermon 120, "The Unity of Divine Being," sec. 7, in Baker, *Works*, 4:62.

6. John Wesley, *Explanatory Notes upon the New Testament* (London: Epworth Press, 1944).

7. E.g., *NT Notes*, Rom. 8:28; Sermon 15, "The Great Assize," sec. 2.10, in Baker, *Works*, 1:365; Sermon 66, "The Signs of the Times," sec. 2.9, in Baker, *Works*, 2:530; Sermon 118, "On the Omnipresence of God," sec. 2.1, in Baker, *Works*, 4:43.

8. As discussed in Randy L. Maddox, *Responsible Grace, John Wesley's Practical Theology* (Nashville: Abingdon Press, 1994), 19.

9. It's debatable whether or not Wesley was fair to his Calvinist critics. Wesley charged that, unless carefully nuanced, predestinarian thinking raises near-blasphemous reservations about the efficacy and the scope of God's love. (At one place in his later thought, Wesley even speculates on the possibility that God's love is so expansive that even animals may be given a place in eternity!)

10. "On the Death of George Whitefield," in Thomas Jackson, ed., *The Works of John Wesley,* 3rd ed. (London: Wesleyan Methodist Book Room, 1872; repr., Grand Rapids, MI: Baker, 1979), 3:1.

11. Albert C. Outler, ed. *John Wesley,* (New York: Oxford University Press, 1964), 101–3.

Further Reading

I was preceded, and even exceeded, in this effort to explicate basic United Methodist beliefs by Bishop Mack B. Stokes, *Major United Methodist Beliefs* (Nashville: Abingdon Press, 1971); and Bishop Emerson Colaw, *Beliefs of a United Methodist Christian* (Nashville: Tidings, 1972). If you want to know more about United Methodist beliefs, see the following:

Abraham, William J. *Wesley for Armchair Theologians.* Louisville, KY: Westminster John Knox Press, 2005.

Campbell, Ted A. *Methodist Doctrine: The Essentials.* Nashville: Abingdon Press, 1999.

Collins, Kenneth J. *A Real Christian: The Life of John Wesley.* Nashville: Abingdon Press, 1999.

Heitzenrater, Richard P. *John Wesley and the People Called Methodists.* Nashville: Abingdon Press, 1994.

Jones, Scott J. *United Methodist Doctrine: The Extreme Center.* Nashville: Abingdon Press, 2002.

Klaiber, Walter, and Manfred Marquardt. *Living Grace: An Outline of United Methodist Theology.* Translated and adapted by J. Steven O'Malley and Ulrike R. M. Guthrie. Nashville: Abingdon Press, 2001.

Langford, Thomas A., ed. *Doctrine and Theology in the United Methodist Church.* Nashville: Kingswood Books/Abingdon Press, 1991.

———. *Practical Divinity: Theology in the Wesleyan Tradition.* Nashville: Abingdon Press, 1983.

Maddox, Randy. *Responsible Grace: John Wesley's Practical Theology.* Nashville: Kingswood Books/Abingdon Press, 1994.

Richey, Russell E. *Marks of Methodism: Theology in Ecclesial Practice.* With Dennis M. Campbell and William B. Lawrence. Nashville: Abingdon Press, 2005.

Runyon, Theodore. *The New Creation: John Wesley's Theology Today.* Nashville: Abingdon Press, 1998.

Willimon, William H. *Why I Am United Methodist.* Nashville: Abingdon Press, 1990.

Index of Names

Index of Scriptural Citations